THE EVOLUTION OF TERRORIST PROPAGANDA: THE PARIS ATTACK AND SOCIAL MEDIA

I0439830

HEARING

BEFORE THE

SUBCOMMITTEE ON TERRORISM,
NONPROLIFERATION, AND TRADE

OF THE

COMMITTEE ON FOREIGN AFFAIRS
HOUSE OF REPRESENTATIVES

ONE HUNDRED FOURTEENTH CONGRESS

FIRST SESSION

JANUARY 27, 2015

Serial No. 114–1

Printed for the use of the Committee on Foreign Affairs

U.S. GOVERNMENT PUBLISHING OFFICE

92–852PDF   WASHINGTON : 2015

For sale by the Superintendent of Documents, U.S. Government Publishing Office
Internet: bookstore.gpo.gov Phone: toll free (866) 512–1800; DC area (202) 512–1800
Fax: (202) 512–2104 Mail: Stop IDCC, Washington, DC 20402–0001

COMMITTEE ON FOREIGN AFFAIRS

EDWARD R. ROYCE, California, *Chairman*

CHRISTOPHER H. SMITH, New Jersey
ILEANA ROS-LEHTINEN, Florida
DANA ROHRABACHER, California
STEVE CHABOT, Ohio
JOE WILSON, South Carolina
MICHAEL T. McCAUL, Texas
TED POE, Texas
MATT SALMON, Arizona
DARRELL E. ISSA, California
TOM MARINO, Pennsylvania
JEFF DUNCAN, South Carolina
MO BROOKS, Alabama
PAUL COOK, California
RANDY K. WEBER SR., Texas
SCOTT PERRY, Pennsylvania
RON DeSANTIS, Florida
MARK MEADOWS, North Carolina
TED S. YOHO, Florida
CURT CLAWSON, Florida
SCOTT DesJARLAIS, Tennessee
REID J. RIBBLE, Wisconsin
DAVID A. TROTT, Michigan
LEE M. ZELDIN, New York
TOM EMMER, Minnesota

ELIOT L. ENGEL, New York
BRAD SHERMAN, California
GREGORY W. MEEKS, New York
ALBIO SIRES, New Jersey
GERALD E. CONNOLLY, Virginia
THEODORE E. DEUTCH, Florida
BRIAN HIGGINS, New York
KAREN BASS, California
WILLIAM KEATING, Massachusetts
DAVID CICILLINE, Rhode Island
ALAN GRAYSON, Florida
AMI BERA, California
ALAN S. LOWENTHAL, California
GRACE MENG, New York
LOIS FRANKEL, Florida
TULSI GABBARD, Hawaii
JOAQUIN CASTRO, Texas
ROBIN L. KELLY, Illinois
BRENDAN F. BOYLE, Pennsylvania

AMY PORTER, *Chief of Staff*   THOMAS SHEEHY, *Staff Director*
JASON STEINBAUM, *Democratic Staff Director*

————

SUBCOMMITTEE ON TERRORISM, NONPROLIFERATION, AND TRADE

TED POE, Texas, *Chairman*

JOE WILSON, South Carolina
DARRELL E. ISSA, California
PAUL COOK, California
SCOTT PERRY, Pennsylvania
REID J. RIBBLE, Wisconsin
LEE M. ZELDIN, New York

WILLIAM KEATING, Massachusetts
BRAD SHERMAN, California
BRIAN HIGGINS, New York
JOAQUIN CASTRO, Texas
ROBIN L. KELLY, Illinois

CONTENTS

THE EVOLUTION OF TERRORIST PROPAGANDA: THE PARIS ATTACK AND SOCIAL MEDIA

TUESDAY, JANUARY 27, 2015

House of Representatives,
Subcommittee on Terrorism, Nonproliferation, and Trade,
Committee on Foreign Affairs,
Washington, DC.

The committee met, pursuant to notice, at 2:30 p.m., in room 2172 Rayburn House Office Building, Hon. Ted Poe (chairman of the subcommittee) presiding.

Mr. POE. The subcommittee will come to order.

Without objection, all members may have 5 days to submit statements, questions and extraneous materials for the record subject to the length and limitation in the rules.

Terrorists' use of social media has exploded over the past several years. Terrorist groups from ISIS to the Taliban use social media platforms to recruit, radicalize, spread propaganda and even raise money.

Section 219 of the Immigration and Nationality Act states that it is unlawful to provide a designated foreign terrorist organization with material support or resources, including any property—tangible or intangible—or services, among them, communication, equipment, and facilities.

If foreign terrorist organizations are using American companies to spread propaganda and raise money, the question that remains is: Is this a violation of American law? That is the question for us today.

I asked the Department of Justice this question directly in August 2012. Their answer? They refused to say, as they put it, in the abstract whether a particular company is violating the law or not under this section. So they didn't give a definitive answer.

American newspapers would have never allowed our enemies in World War II to place ads in, say, the New York Times for recruitment of people to go and fight against America. So why do social media companies allow terrorist content on their platforms?

Terrorists know the benefit of social media. Social media is easy to use, it is free, and it reaches everyone in the world. We have seen this most recently with the attacks in Paris; and after the attack, terrorists and their supporters took to social media to praise the attack, recruit new jihadists and fund-raise.

Twitter has become one of the terrorists most popular platforms. As you can see here on the monitor—I believe we have the monitors ready—a British jihadi in Syria is bragging about ISIS and is threatening America.

We have another example of that. Here is an example of terrorists' use of social media. It is a Facebook fan page for Khorasan Group in Syria complete with a message board and photos.

The Khorasan Group is a group set up by al-Qaeda and Syria to specifically attack the United States and Europe. In April 2013, the al-Qaeda branch in Yemen known as AQIM held an online press conference on Twitter, allowing users to submit questions that were answered by the terror group and posted back on Twitter the following week.

In February 2014, a Saudi cleric launched a fund-raising drive on Twitter for jihadists in Syria. The rise of the lone wolf terrorism in recent years has been in part fueled by terrorists' use of social media.

The Boston bombers made two pressure cooker bombs. The recipes for those bombs were published before the attack in al-Qaeda's Inspire magazine. That magazine was released and promoted on social media.

Some people make the excuse that there is no point in shutting down a social media account because it will pop again. But that is not always true. For years, Twitter was asked to shut down an account of the designated foreign terrorist organization, al-Shabaab, which pledged allegiance to al-Qaeda.

In 2013, al-Shabaab live tweeted its attack on the Westgate Mall in Kenya that killed 72 people. Twitter then shut down the account. Al-Shabaab tried to reopen accounts on Twitter but after getting shut down by Twitter each time, it finally quit.

Twitter is far worse than its peers about proactively finding and removing terrorist content. One of our witnesses wrote in late 2013 that the gap between Twitter's practices and industry standards is large enough to raise the specter of negligence.

YouTube is a popular platform for jihadists as well. Videos are especially effective in attracting and funding and donations. Every major video released by al-Qaeda is uploaded to YouTube and, as soon as they are released, to jihadist forums.

ISIS posts videos on YouTube in a service called Vimeo that depict graphic violence. However, YouTube does try to remove them but can't get them all.

In September 2010, I did send a letter to YouTube urging them to change their policy when it came to terrorist accounts. They did, allowing any user to flag a video for terrorist content, but have since changed that policy and instead take videos down if they post graphic content or train terrorists.

Facebook is also a favorite social media site for terrorists and jihadists. Fortunately, Facebook has redoubled its efforts to proactively identify and remove that content.

In 2011, the White House published a counter radicalization strategy that acknowledged terrorists' use of the Internet and social media to spread hate and violence. The report also committed the administration to devising a strategy to deal with this phenomena. However, no such strategy has been published by the administration.

Then I sent a letter with a number of other colleagues in September 2012 urging the FBI to do more to reduce terrorists' use of Twitter. The FBI refused, saying they gained intelligence about groups and individuals from their social media activity, even though it is apparent that this social media activity recruits terrorists who want to kill.

That may be true, but it must be weighed against the benefits of terrorist groups that enjoy this use because of the activity.

The debate should take place and it should inform our policies about how to deal with this threat. At the very least we need a strategy, and that is the purpose—one of the purposes of this hearing.

I will now yield 5 minutes to the new ranking member, Mr. Keating from Massachusetts, for his opening comments.

Mr. KEATING. Thank you, Mr. Chairman.

Let me start off by thanking you for holding this important hearing and a timely hearing at that. Further, I would like to note this is indeed my first subcommittee hearing as ranking member and I look forward to working with you in the future.

We begin this Congress with news of the terrible shootings in Paris. Our condolences continue to be with the friends and families of those victims and with all those who have been impacted similarly by senseless tragedies in Boston, New York, Brussels, Sydney, Peshawar, Nairobi and, unfortunately, the list can go on and on.

This month's heartbreaking and gruesome attacks against Charlie Hebdo and Hyper Cacher market in Paris have resoundingly brought people together from across the Atlantic and from all walks of life to express their strong commitment to pluralistic, democratic and tolerant societies.

Yet, the same space in which terrorists and criminals operate to recruit and radicalize like-minded or just plain hateful individuals in the same medium is indeed the same democratic type of medium where open societies exercise their very freedoms, the kind of freedoms that these extremists abhor.

There is no doubt that social networking, the Internet and propaganda have become the premier recruitment and radicalization tools for terrorist gangs and those expanding their reach far into Europe and the United States.

This leads to a problem where the simplest quickest strategies to eliminate this type of harmful influence can also compromise the very basis of a free society, in effect complementing the terrorists' cause.

In a recent report issued by the bipartisan Policy Center, two former co-chairs of the 9–11 Commission argue that while

> "the use of Internet to radicalize and recruit homegrown terrorists is the single most important and dangerous innovation since the terrorist attacks of September 11, 2001. Approaches that are aimed at reducing the supply of violent extremist content on the Internet are neither feasible or desirable."

While advocating for the government to retain its capability for aggressive take downs of foreign-based Web sites to stop a terrorist attack, the report recommends a strategy of building partnerships with Internet companies, the private sector foundations, philanthropists and community groups to build capacity and to help potentially credible messengers such as mainstream groups, victims of terrorism and other stakeholders to become a more effective in advocating and conveying their messages.

As a former district attorney, I too have seen the profound effect of working to raise the voices of those within communities across the U.S. that work toward peace and multicultural acceptance.

While we debate ways in which to balance security needs in a free society, it is important to revisit our counter terrorism strategies to ensure that they are adequately incorporating the role of modern technology and communications.

As I mentioned earlier, there is a larger piece of this puzzle, and that is the mind set of militants who come from Western nations to join brutal gangs that go on to rape, kill and divide thousands if not millions.

As a transatlantic community, we can only fight the lure of terrorism by determining its causes and devising appropriate counter measures. In particular, I feel the messages promoting the heritage and very cultural history of the Mideast and North Africa will be important to help young people define their true identities instead of listening to backwoods propaganda seeking to destroy this history.

Today, radicalization, online or otherwise, is occurring across the world in rural and urban settings, wealthy and poor communities and among all educational levels.

In the long run, we must ensure that the course of action we pursue not only targets terrorist groups but the polarizing policies that often lead to societal division, and to do this, a balance between security and liberties must be maintained.

The subject of today's hearing is of the utmost concern to our national security and I look forward to hearing from our witnesses and thank them for being here and their perspectives on this timely issue.

Thank you, Mr. Chairman. I will yield back my time.

Mr. POE. I thank the gentleman.

The Chair will recognize other members for their 1-minute opening statement. The Chair recognizes the gentleman from California, Colonel Cook, for 1 minute.

Mr. COOK. Thank you, Mr. Chairman.

I want to compliment you on having this hearing. As somebody who has been characterized as being born in Jurassic Park, this is a hearing which, I don't know how many years ago—10 years ago, what have you—didn't have a clue what was going on and, unfortunately, there is a lot of Americans that still do not understand social media and the importance of it.

I am also somebody that spent a long time in the military, read all the books and everything else including Sun Tsu about knowing your enemy, and this new enemy that we have, international terrorism, which every week, every day something horrible happens and they are using a weapons system that, unfortunately, I and many of my colleagues were very, very naive in understanding this.

I have had an education the last few years or I wouldn't be here. We all use it now. I think everybody in this room uses social media and it is something that young people they listen to, the 30-second, the 15-second sound bite, even a minute, and it is almost addictive.

And, obviously, our enemies are enemies of democracy. They have used this so effectively in recruiting and finding out exactly how to get to people and using it as a strategy against us.

So I actually believe we are going to need more of these hearings. Unfortunately, a lot of our colleagues couldn't make it. But this is the wave of the future because it works, unfortunately.

So thank you again for having this very timely hearing. I yield back.

Mr. POE. Gentleman yields back his time. The Chair will recognize the former ranking member of this subcommittee, the gentleman from California, Mr. Sherman.

Mr. SHERMAN. Judge, Bill, I am very much looking forward to working with you on the subcommittee in this Congress. I should point out that this subcommittee came into existence in 2003 and for 12 years I have been either chair or ranking member of this subcommittee.

It began as the Subcommittee on Terrorism, Nonproliferation and Human Rights. Two years later, the human rights part was transferred to another subcommittee. Then in the 110th Congress as well as the 111th, I was able to serve as chair of the subcommittee and persuade then-Chairman Lantos to add the economic jurisdiction of the full committee to this subcommittee, dealing with trade promotion, dealing with trade licensing and other limits on exports.

And so I look forward to this next 2 years with the chair, the ranking member and all the members of the subcommittee.

As to the matter at hand, I look forward to hearing from our witnesses on not only how we can be on defense and take down the bad stuff, but how we can be on offense and use social media and traditional media to get our message out.

As to taking down the bad stuff, that is what First Amendment lawyers would call prior restraint if we did it through government fiat. So among our possible policies are to simply name and shame and nudge these Internet publishers, if you will, to take down the bad stuff.

If we want to go further and use the power of the state to take down information, I think it is incumbent on Congress to craft a new statute defining what the responsibilities of these Internet companies are, and I yield back.

Mr. POE. I thank the gentleman.

I will introduce the witnesses that we have before us today and then they will each be allowed to give us 5 minutes of their testimony.

Ambassador Mark Wallace is the CEO of the Counter Extremism Project. He is a former U.S. Ambassador to the United Nations. Prior to his political work, practiced law as a commercial litigation attorney.

Mr. J.M. Berger is an author and analyst studying extremism. He is also the founder of the Web site IntelWire.com, which publishes investigative journalism, analysis, and primary source documents on terrorism and international security.

Mr. Evan Kohlmann is the chief information officer at Flashpoint Partners where he focuses on innovation and product development. Mr. Kohlmann has served as a consultant in terrorism matters to various government and law enforcement agencies throughout the world.

Ms. Rebecca MacKinnon is the director of the Ranking Digital Rights program at New America. She is the co-founder of Global Voices Online and author of the book, "Consent of the Networked: The Worldwide Struggle for Internet Freedom."

The Chair now will recognize Ambassador Wallace. We will start with you. You have 5 minutes.

STATEMENT OF THE HONORABLE MARK WALLACE, CHIEF EXECUTIVE OFFICER, COUNTER EXTREMISM PROJECT

Mr. WALLACE. Chairman Poe, Ranking Member Keating and members of the subcommittee, thank you for the opportunity to testify on the hijacking and weaponization of social media by extremist groups to radicalize and recruit new members and to plan violent attacks against innocent people.

The evidence of social media's reach can be seen in the thousands of people who continue to pour into Syria and Iraq in response to online propaganda by radical extremist groups and the grim aftermath of terror attacks that bear witness to the power of social media to radicalize and encourage violence.

This hearing can lead to a better understanding of the growing problem of social media abuse and a more coordinated and cooperative relationship between technology companies like Twitter and those who want to stop extremists from anonymously abusing social media platforms.

American companies have led the world in revolutionary online technology and social media. Unfortunately, these open platforms are also the tools of choice to spread messages of hate and for extremist groups like ISIS to propagandize, radicalize, recruit and commit cyber jihad.

A major focus of the Counter Extremism Project's work is to combat extremist recruitment, rhetoric and calls for acts of terror online, starting with Twitter.

Through our crowd sourcing campaign, #CEPDigitalDisruption, we have researched and reported hundreds of extremists to Twitter and to law enforcement. The question today is whether or not companies like Twitter will partner to combat those extremists who hijack and weaponize social media for terror.

We have reached out in the spirit of cooperation to Twitter. The response we get from Twitter is dismissive to the point of dereliction. A Twitter official has said publically that "one man's terrorist is another man's freedom fighter."

This statement is insipid and unserious. Social media sites have a responsibility to act against extremists. An American-born jihadi from Minneapolis operates on Twitter with the alias Mujahid Miski.

He is one of the most influential jihadis using Twitter and has tweeted some of the most heinous content we have seen, including threats to behead CEP's president, the former Homeland Security adviser, Fran Townsend.

He boasted he has been suspended from Twitter 20 times and keeps coming back, yet Twitter does nothing to remove his new accounts. As a result, we have been playing a never ending game of Whac-A-Mole in trying to stop him.

We have raised these issues to Twitter. Twitter has not taken further action against him. I respectfully request that a copy of the tweets we have reported over the course of our digital disruption campaign be included along with my prepared testimony as part of this hearing's record.

Mr. POE. Without objection, it will be made part of the record.

Mr. WALLACE. Thank you, sir.

I would like to clarify why our focus is on Twitter. In the case of jihadis online, Twitter is the gateway drug. This is where vulnerable people are first exposed to radical content. From Twitter, the conversation moves to platforms like AskFM, where those being recruited can ask questions, for example: What is life like in ISIS, or how can I get to Syria?

Then the conversation moves to private chat applications like Kick or WhatsApp. The path I just described is not fictional. It is exactly how three Denver girls were radicalized and tried to join ISIS.

We must stop recruitment at the gateway, Twitter. We stand ready to work with governments and any company in finding the right mix of remedies that effectively attacks this growing problem while protecting our values and liberties.

There are immediate actions that Twitter should take. Twitter should grant trusted reporting status to governments and groups like ours to swiftly identify and ensure Twitter's expeditious removal of extremists online.

The reporting process on Twitter is long and cumbersome. A more accessible reporting protocol should be added for users to report suspected extremist activity.

America's leading tech company should adopt a policy statement that extremist activities will not be tolerated—simple but important.

Twitter has a system where people can verify their accounts. This concept can be the foundation for a tiered system whereby unverified accounts are restricted and subject to streamlined review.

When one of the most influential and pro-ISIS Twitter accounts, ShamiWitness, was publically revealed to be an Indian businessman, it shook the cyber jihadi network. He immediately stopped his online jihad.

Twitter should reveal detailed information, including the names and locations of the most egregious cyber jihadis. We can collectively agree that the most egregious of cyber jihadis do not deserve anonymity or the right to engage in hate and incitement of terror speech.

The FBI shut down Silk Road. There are other enforcement successes: Online drug distribution, child pornography, tobacco sales and sex trafficking, among others. If we can confront these activities there are strategies that we can use on those who hijack and weaponize social media.

Thank you, Chairman Poe, Ranking Member Keating and members of the subcommittee, and I would just like to introduce Alan Goldsmith, Jen Lach, Darlene Cayabyab and Steven Cohen who are really the brains of the operation because it depends on young people to understand these complicated networks. I just wanted to introduce them.

[The prepared statement of Mr. Wallace follows:]

Testimony before the House Foreign Affairs Committee

Subcommittee on Terrorism, Nonproliferation, and Trade

January 27, 2015

The Honorable Mark D. Wallace

CEO, Counter Extremism Project

Chairman Poe, Ranking Member Keating and members of the Subcommittee, thank you for the opportunity to appear before you today to discuss what could be the most pressing public safety and national security issue today: the hijacking and weaponization of social media platforms by extremist groups to radicalize and recruit new members, and plan violent attacks against innocent people around the world. The evidence of social media's reach can be seen in the thousands of citizens from Western countries who continue to pour into Syria and Iraq in response to unrelenting and slickly produced propaganda by ISIS and other radical extremist groups; and the grim aftermath of lone wolf attacks, most recently in Canada and Australia, that bear witness to the power of social media to radicalize and encourage violence against Western targets.

The Counter Extremism Project (CEP), is a not-for-profit, non-partisan, international policy organization whose mission is to combat the growing threat from extremist ideology. Led by a renowned group of former world leaders and former diplomats, including former U.S. Homeland Security Advisor Frances Townsend and Senator Joseph I. Lieberman, CEP's mission is to combat extremism by pressuring financial support networks, countering the narrative of extremists and their online recruitment and calls for terror, and serving as a resource for best practices laws, policies and regulations.

CEP is assembling what we hope will be the world's most extensive research database on extremist groups and their networks of support, mapping the social and financial networks, tools and methodologies and providing an indispensable resource to governments, media, NGOs and the public. Modeled in part on advocacy efforts to counter Iran's efforts to acquire nuclear weapons, CEP exposes shadowy channels of financial support to extremist groups and brings to bear private and public sector pressure to disrupt them.

We use the latest communications tools to expose the threat of extremists and to mount a global counter-narrative to directly counter extremist ideology. Our efforts are focused

1

particularly on young people in communities across the globe vulnerable to extremist messaging and recruitment.

We commend this Subcommittee for recognizing the importance and the timeliness of this issue – an issue on which our Western allies, especially Great Britain have led.

We hope that this hearing can lead to a better understanding of the growing problem of social media abuse and hopefully, to a more coordinated and cooperative relationship between technology companies like Twitter and those of us who want to stop extremists from anonymously abusing social media platforms to expand their power and propel their declared war on Western society, institutions, values and culture.

Over the past two decades, the United States has led the world in advances in online technology and social media. We are the country that invented Google, Twitter, Facebook, YouTube and Instagram – all of which have revolutionized the way we communicate with each other globally, the way we share knowledge and ideas, and the way information is spread. These digital platforms have been a colossal force in empowering individuals and shining a light on abuses of power.

Unfortunately, these open platforms are also the tools of choice to spread messages of hate, creating a dark playground for extremist groups like ISIS to propagandize, radicalize, recruit new members and commit cyber jihad in the form of broadcasted beheadings, stoning's, cyber-attacks and encouraging DOS attacks and data hackings.

The reality is that extremists have been more agile, aggressive and insidious in their use of social platforms than governments have been in tracking, stopping and preventing them from hijacking the online world.

The Wilson Center's "New Terrorism & New Media" report found that 90 percent of terrorist activity taking place online today utilize social networking tools: 90 percent. According to the report, "these forums act as a virtual firewall to help safeguard the identities of those who participate, and they offer subscribers a chance to make direct contact with terrorist representatives, to ask questions, and even to contribute and help out the cyber-jihad."

Social media provides extremists with easily accessible and far-reaching platforms through which to deliver their dangerous messages. Their use of digital media has been so successful, so widespread and so encouraged that leading jihadist forums al-Fida and Shumukh al-Islam published the following regarding cyber-jihad:

Any Muslim who intends to do jihad against the enemy electronically, is considered in one way or another a mujaheed, as long as he meets the conditions of jihad such as the sincere intention and the goal of serving Islam and defending it, even if he is far away from the battlefield.

That statement is emblematic of the new and troubling chapter in the sophisticated use of digital technologies by extremist groups, allowing them to spread far beyond discrete physical geographies to reach broader audiences worldwide.

During the past year, ISIS in particular has deployed an incredibly sophisticated social media campaign to radicalize and recruit new members and to call for acts of terror around the world. A major focus of CEP's work is to combat the rampant extremist recruitment, rhetoric and calls for acts of terror online, starting with Twitter. Through a rigorous research and crowdsourcing campaign called #CEPDigitalDisruption, we have identified and reported hundreds of extremists to Twitter. To be clear, our standard is incitement of violence and direct threats rooted in our American constitutional jurisprudence or free speech. Over the past three months, we've monitored hundreds of accounts and exposed the violent calls to action and instances of direct threats against individuals that jihadis are propagating on Twitter.

Even with our sacred protections of speech, our legal system does not protect certain forms of speech that crosses lines of public safety, and national security. Regrettably, as extremists have hijacked and weaponized social media platforms we are at a moment of collision between the good and thoughtful people who seek an unfettered and uninhibited right to speech through social media and similarly good and thoughtful people who seek to protect us from those who use social media platforms as an essential tool of terror.

We have seen these collisions before of course. Inevitably, public outrage over the terrible acts of the relative few who employ protected rights for perverse reasons leads to limitations through laws and regulations.

Private enterprise and businesses that profit from new technologies can either be a partner or an adversary. The question now before us is whether or not companies like Twitter will thoughtfully partner to combat those extremists who hijack and weaponize social media for terror.

As a private-sector non-profit organization whose mission is combatting extremism, we have reached out in the spirit of cooperation to Twitter in an effort to stop extremists who encourage and instruct in the ways of murder and terror, from abusing the platform.

And yet the response we get from Twitter is dismissive to the point of dereliction. We have written three letters describing the problem and requesting a sit-down between Twitter and CEP leadership. Twitter has ignored all but one letter, and its reply, simply put, was dismissive at best.

Twitter's dismissiveness on the issue of violent extremists who have hijacked and weaponized its platform can be best summarized in a quote given to Mother Jones magazine by a Twitter official: "One man's terrorist is another man's freedom fighter." Of course this statement is insipid and unserious, particularly in the context of al Qaeda, ISIS and many others. We strongly disagree with Twitter. The hijacking and weaponization of its platform is a dangerous and growing problem. We believe social media sites have a responsibility to more than protect their bottom line -- they have a responsibility to act against abuse. They provide the means for violent extremists and there should be appropriate accountability.

A great example of Twitter's failure to combat the threat of violent extremism online can be seen in a man named Mohamed Abdullahi Hassan — an American born jihadi from Minneapolis, Minnesota who is under federal indictment in Minneapolis and wanted by the FBI for joining a terrorist organization. He goes by the alias Mujahid Miski on Twitter. Miski is not only one of the most influential jihadis using Twitter to spread propaganda and recruit, he has also been responsible for tweeting some of the most heinous, violent content we've seen — including threats to behead our organization's President, Fran Townsend, and calling for every Muslim to kill one Jew in order to eradicate the Jewish people.

He boasts in his Twitter biography that he's been suspended from Twitter 20 times and keeps coming back, yet Twitter does nothing to monitor or remove his new accounts, despite the fact that each is similar to the one preceding it. As a result of Twitter's bad practice, we have been playing a never-ending game of whack-a-mole. We've raised these issues to Twitter through various channels — we've reported Miski's account over and over, we've written letters, gone to the press, and yet Twitter has not taken further action to end his abuse of its platform.

I respectfully request that the committee accept as part of this hearing's record a copy of the tweets we've reported over the course of our Digital Disruption campaign.

I would like to clarify why our focus is on Twitter versus other social media networks. When discussing the problem of drug abuse, Marijuana is often referred to as a gateway drug. In the case of jihadis online — Twitter is the gateway drug. This is where vulnerable individuals (usually young people) are first exposed to propaganda and radical content. This content is extremely accessible and public and Twitter is the introductory point to this world. From there, the conversation moves to a platform like AskFM where those being recruited can ask more in-depth questions -- for example, "What life will be like as a part of ISIS?" and "How can I get to Syria?" From there, the conversation moves to private chat applications like Kik or WhatsApp. By the time the conversation gets to the point of Kik/WhatsApp and even AskFM in many cases, it's too late. We need to stop recruitment at its gateway, and without question, Twitter is that gateway. This scenario is not fictional, it is exactly how three Denver girls were radicalized and were almost successful in joining ISIS in Syria.

In the past four months, there have been terror attacks carried out in Canada, the United States, Australia and France in the name of radical Islam. In two of these cases, Canada and

Australia, there is undisputed evidence that the attack was perpetrated by a jihadi who was using social media – either to spread content pushed out by others, or to leave messages and post justifications for his actions. If this isn't direct evidence of the extreme danger that comes from allowing these activities to take place uninhibited online, then we are simply hiding our heads in the sand.

This problem cannot be overcome by wishing it away. The number of Twitter abusers is admittedly very small in relation to the number of users, which is an even more powerful and compelling justification for taking action.

We believe strongly that there are very concrete actions that can help prevent extremists from using online tools for terror. Our goal cannot simply be to investigate, draw conclusions and count the bodies after the carnage has already taken place. Our goal should be to prevent murder, injury and destruction. And more broadly, there is a challenge for many parties in providing a counter-narrative that is more compelling and empowering than the hatred we're discussing today. But as a practical matter, while we go after the extremists, we cannot simply pretend that social media companies are helpless. They are not. They should — and they must — take a more active role in preventing extremist access to their platforms, pulling down accounts of extremists and keeping them down. We should all urge and as necessary compel social media companies to act responsibility.

If Twitter can beef up its policies as it relates to bullying and harassment of women, why does it show such dismissiveness when it comes to those promoting and glorifying terror? We stand ready to work with the Congress, the Administration and any company in finding the right mix of remedies that effectively attacks this growing problem, while protecting our values and liberties. But it must be attacked – and now.

The war against ISIS Al Qaeda and other extremist actors has many fronts – and an important one is online. While we undertake air strikes and other military responses to combat them, nothing is being done on a large scale to counter the narrative of extremists and fight back against them online.

Our concern is that we've seen a real evolution in the sophistication of methods utilized by ISIS and other extremist groups in the past year. Many ISIS members, sympathizers and supporters are young people. They've grown up in a digital world. They are digital natives, and they know how to use digital media to their advantage. They prey on at risk youths in the same way that gangs prey on at-risk kids in bad neighborhoods. And their tactics are escalating.

Several months ago, CEP as well as a large number of our supporters were targeted by a malware attack. More recently, a U.S. newspaper, and a Maryland television station were taken over by supporters of ISIS, as was the Twitter page of U.S. Central Command. This is completely unacceptable. We have called several times for the establishment of a National Cyber Terrorism Center – and we were pleased with President Obama's call during the State of the Union address for Congress to pass legislation to deal with this same issue. But cyberattacks are but one part of the issue – we need to deal with the abuse of technology platforms directly and effectively as part of a broader effort to combat violent extremism rooting and spreading online.

There is an urgent need for social platforms to take action to stop extremists from abusing their sites to spread terrorist propaganda, recruit new members and kill innocent civilians. Government, private organizations like CEP, and companies like Twitter must work together to identify and counter the violent narrative of extremists and their recruitment efforts.

We have outlined below three clear and immediate changes that Twitter could make that would go toward stemming some of the issues outlined in this testimony:

- **Trusted Reporting Status on Twitter** – one of the problems we've encountered in the #CEPDigitalDisruption campaign is that accounts we report go into a long queue and are not immediately addressed. By giving CEP, as well as other agencies like the State Department, trusted reporting status and opening a direct line of communication between CEP and social networks, we can more easily and swiftly identify and remove the most notorious extremists online.

- **Streamlined Reporting Process** – Our campaign relies in part on our audience to report accounts along with CEP. A roadblock we run into is that the reporting process on Twitter is long and cumbersome, and weeks can pass before action occurs. Twitter has recently begun a new reporting process for women who are being harassed online, so those complaints are dealt with more quickly, but when we try to take down a violent extremist, the request falls into a catchall category that includes reporting spam. We believe that a new reporting protocol should be added for users to report suspected terrorist/extremist activity as a way to speed the process.

- **Clear, Public Policy on Extremism** –While each organization will have to take a somewhat different approach to combat the unique ways extremists are using each platform, we believe that showing a united front among America's most important tech companies is of critical importance to fighting violent extremism. This includes a clear, public, policy statement that extremist activities will not be tolerated, and that organizations like Twitter and Google, along with CEP, will work tirelessly to identify and remove content. All social networks and technology companies should actively identify these persons and ban them swiftly.

- **Verified Accounts** – Extremists flaunt even the minimal efforts Twitter has made to enforce its own standards. Once banned, they come back minutes later with new accounts, like Miski has done over and over. They often self-identify as ISIS, jihadists and terrorists, and use names similar to their deactivated accounts to make it easier to recreate their networks in short order. Twitter already has a system where people can verify their accounts, meaning they have self-identified and those carry a small blue visible check mark. We believe this concept can be the foundation for a tiered system whereby unverified accounts are restricted and subject to a streamlined system of review for prohibited content.

- **Technology as the Solution** – Those of us who believe in free speech, pluralism, peace and tolerance will not abide forever a circumstance where the right to freely and anonymously threaten, incite, and coordinate terror is protected to a higher degree than the lives of innocent victims. I do not have any problem with someone criticizing me in an intemperate way on Twitter. I don't like it, mind you, but it's a right I respect and defend. But when someone threatens to kill, or urges countless other anonymous individuals to do so, that crosses the line into abuse of the platform. There is a technological solution out there that I think most Twitter users would accept as a fair tradeoff for lives saved. Whether the solution to this problem is defined by Twitter or defined for Twitter is not the most important question. The most important question is will this come in time to prevent an attack in the U.S. like we just saw in France?

- **The Bright Spotlight of Transparency on the Most Egregious Extremist Accounts** -- When the United Kingdom's Chanel 4 revealed that one of the most influential and pro-ISIS Twitter accounts, ShamiWitness, belonged to Bangalore, India businessman Mehdi Masroor Biswas, it shook up the cyber-jihadi network. Once revealed, Biswas immediately stopped his egregious online support for Syrian and Iraqi Jihadis. The ShamiWitness Twitter account had 17,000 followers, including many of the Islamist foreign fighters active on social media. We believe that Twitter should reveal detailed information – including names -- of the most egregious of the cyber-jihad terror actors who are the foundation of the online jihad architecture. The bright spotlight will assuredly have a further disruptive effect on other cyber-jihad account holders like ShamiWitness. By calling out these seed accounts, Twitter can play a crucial role in shutting them down. Of course, the most aggressive defenders of the anonymous and "right to tweet" will chafe at such a suggestion and they should be heard. But surely, we can collectively agree that these most egregious of cyber-jihadis do not deserve anonymity or the right of free hate and incitement of terror speech through the use of Twitter.

CEP is also developing concepts that we hope with the advent of new technologies will make it much more difficult for the worst of extremists to hide in the anonymity of the online world. Our focus is that the worst actors can be brought to justice while protecting the rights of the many users of such platforms who employ them for legitimate expressions of free speech. We have faced such challenges before and have employed technology to confront them.

What many social media companies overlook is that the business imperative for them to act cooperatively is great. With each successive and horrific misuse of social media the outcry for limitations will be greater and greater. Working in an adversarial way is not only morally wrong but will also increase the cost of doing business.

CEP is not alone in calling out social media companies to do more in this area. In a recent article in the Guardian, English Prime Minister David Cameron issued a plea to US internet giants to accept they have a social responsibility to help fight terrorism by allowing Britain's intelligence agencies access to the data and content of online communications between terror suspects. And in a subsequent interview with ITV News, Mr. Cameron said he would ask President Obama to step up pressure on web companies such as Twitter and Facebook to do more to cooperate with the intelligence agencies as they seek to track terror suspects.

I would point out that while Twitter has been non-responsive, other Internet and social media companies like YouTube have instituted reforms – such as instituting trusted reporting status for government agencies – as a means of combatting serious instances of abuse without interfering with or inconveniencing subscribers.

Successfully combatting extremist activities online need not be an insurmountable challenge. The Federal Bureau of Investigation shut down Silk Road, an online "Darknet" market trading in Bitcoin (BTC) currency, primarily used for selling illegal drugs, but also for child pornography, weapons, counterfeit passports and money, and even for contract killers to solicit clients. Silk Road users could browse and trade anonymously (to a very high degree), with a very low risk of detection. But the FBI pinpointed the foreign server that ran Silk Road despite its use of anonymity software to protect its location, and obtained records from the server's hosting provider.

That is one success story, but there are others involving investigation and prosecution of online drug distribution, child pornography, tobacco sales, and sex trafficking.

This is a quote from FBI agent Gilbert Trill following a successful sting operation into online sex trafficking.

"Some child predators mistakenly believe the anonymity of cyberspace shields them from scrutiny. In fact, their use of the Internet gives us new tools in our efforts to investigate this insidious behavior."

I am convinced that if we can make progress against these types of criminal activities, there are strategies that we can bring to bear on those who attempt to hijack and weaponize social media. We must join Prime Minister Cameron, along with our other allies around the world in recognizing the impact of this activity and implementing ways to stop it.

As I said earlier, all of these marvelous communications tools were invented in the United States. We have a duty to lead in finding ways to ensure the safety and security of our nation and our allies.

Thank you Mr. Chairman, Ranking Member Keating and all the members of this subcommittee.

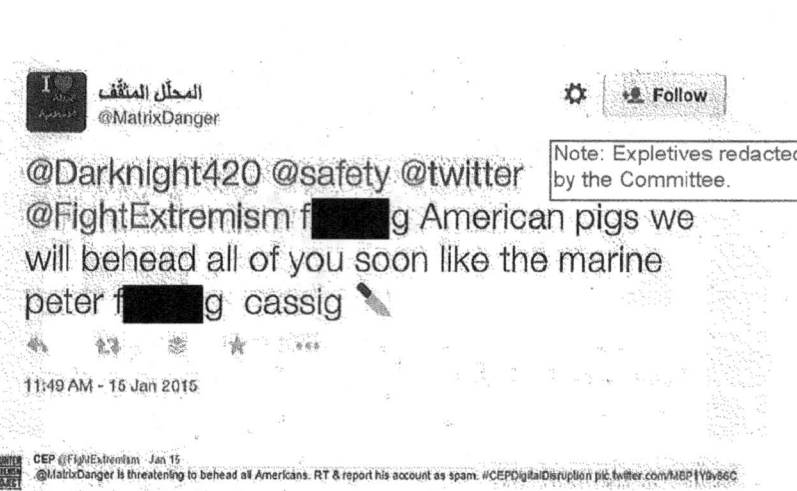

المحلّل المثقّف
@MatrixDanger

Note: Expletives redacted by the Committee.

@Darknight420 @safety @twitter @FightExtremism f████g American pigs we will behead all of you soon like the marine peter f███g cassig 🔪

11:49 AM - 15 Jan 2015

CEP @FightExtremism · Jan 15
@MatrixDanger is threatening to behead all Americans. RT & report his account as spam. #CEPDigitalDisruption pic.twitter.com/MBP1Y9v86C

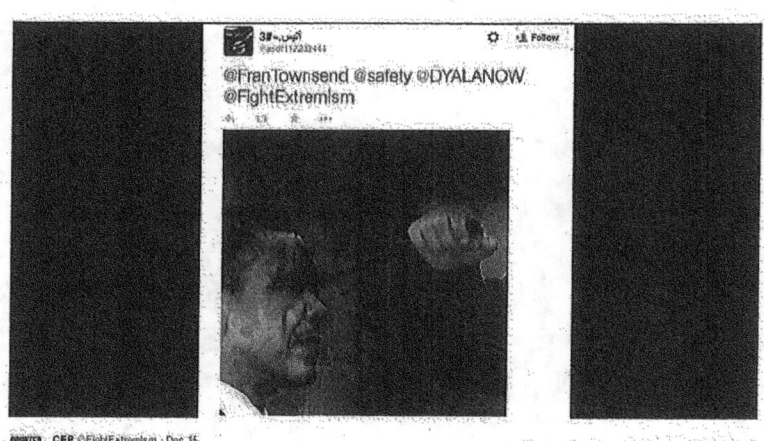

CEP @FightExtremism · Dec 15
@Twitter has an obligation to remove @barackobama assassination threats. RT if you agree. #CEPDigitalDisruption pic.twitter.com/hg0cjQiKG3z

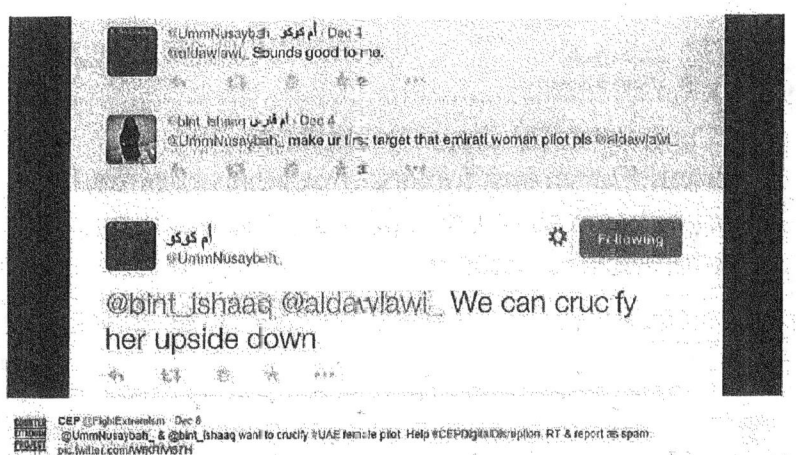

@UmmNusaybah_ أم كركر · Dec 4
@aldawlawi_ Sounds good to me.

bint_Ishaaq أم قارس · Dec 4
@UmmNusaybah_ make ur first target that emirati woman pilot pls @aldawlawi_

أم كركر
@UmmNusaybah_

⚙ Following

@bint_Ishaaq @aldawlawi_ We can crucify
her upside down

CEP @FightExtremism · Dec 8
@UmmNusaybah_ & @bint_Ishaaq want to crucify #UAE female pilot. Help #CEPDigitalDisruption. RT & report as spam:
pic.twitter.com/WiKitM6TH
↩ ♺ 12 ⭐ 2

Mujahid Miski
@Muhajir___1924

Follow

I heard the #IslamicState captured a #Jewish
female POW in #Kobane, Aynul Islam.
I cant wait to see her slaughtered.
لله الله في الذبح

CEP @FightExtremism · Dec 2
@Muhajir___1924 wants to slaughter female, Jewish captive. RT & report as spam to @Twitter #CEPDigitalDisruption
pic.twitter.com/4Voomt8kH0
↩ ♺ 13 ⭐ 2

Mujahid Miski @The_Minnesotan4 · 8h
Allahu Akbar Twitter Jihadis. Wallahi you've made the kuffs cry. Read& Reweet this InshaAllah
buzzfeed.com/hayesbrown/tur...

@JizyaCollectCO أين النجم · 8h
@The_Minnesotan4 lol gettin them frustrated eh Akhi

Mujahid Miski
@The_Minnesotan4   ⚙ ＋ Follow

@JizyaCollectCO Alhamdulillah akhi, our whole life is about getting them frustrated or beheaded. #baaqiyah

FAVORITE
1

3:51 AM · 19 Nov 2014

CEP @FightExtremism · Nov 19
@safety @FBI- @The_Minnesotan4 is threatening to behead fmr @WhiteHouse Advisor @FranTownsend #CEPDigitalDisruption pic.twitter.com/XNXsibMfl7

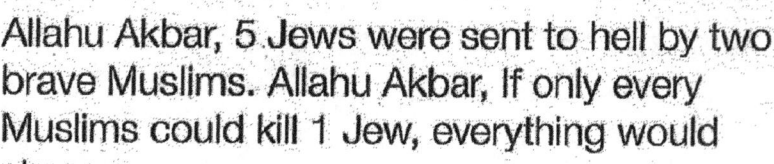

Mujahid Miski
@The_Minnesotan3   ⚙ Following

Allahu Akbar, 5 Jews were sent to hell by two brave Muslims. Allahu Akbar, If only every Muslims could kill 1 Jew, everything would change.

CEP @FightExtremism · Nov 18
@AmbShapiro: @The_Minnesotan3 is calling for killing of Jews. Help us? RT & report as spam. #CEPDigitalDisruption pic.twitter.com/uFfye2741O

Abu Ramzi Ashami
@greenbird70_72

✿ +👤 Follow

James Foley ✔
Steven Sotloff ✔
David Haines ✔
Alan Henning ✔
Peter Kassig ✔
Obama Loading.......

Nothing is imposible with Allah

CEP @FightExtremism · Nov 17
ATTN @Twitter: @greenbird70_72 says @BarackObama is the next westerner to be beheaded. #CEPDigitalDisruption
pic.twitter.com/mVB4nvryA0

أبو إسماعيل
@ShamBreaking5

✿ +👤 Follow

Today it is Peter Kassig...

Tomorrow it will be Barack Obama.

#MTVStars #ZDRSEDK4 #BlindsPH

CEP @FightExtremism · Nov 17
.@ShamBreaking5 tweets pic of Kassig beheading, says @BarackObama next. @SecretService #CEPDigitalDisruption
pic.twitter.com/4OpkrcWhoW

ابو عنتر
@abu3antarr
⚙ 👤 Follow

#no2shia we're coming for your necks. I want to behead that lebo fag with he's own knife.

↩ ↻ ★ •••

FAVORITE
1

11:56 AM - 13 Sep 2014

CEP @FightExtremism · Nov 10
Hey @Twitter - @Abu3Antarr is threatening murder of #Shia & gays. Will you remove him? #CEPDigitalDisruption pic.twitter.com/vRobbaYHrj

↩ ↻ 5 ★ •••

Ghazi
@ghazi_dimashqi
⚙ 👤 Follow

I advocate the complete and utter genocide of Kufr.

↩ ↻ ★ •••

RETWEETS
2

8:42 AM - 4 Nov 2014

CEP @FightExtremism · Nov 4
Hey @Twitter - @Ghazi_Dimashqi advocates the genocide of all non-muslims. Will you remove him? #CEPDigitalDisruption pic.twitter.com/hvO6ljrwgh

↩ ↻ 0 ★ 3 •••

Black Hawk
@Blackhawk21974

⚙  Following

1000 ASIANS COMING IN TO JOIN IS & FIGHT US. MORE ARE COMING. SOON NO AMERICANS CAN WALK SAFELY IN ASIAN COUNTRIES COZ THEY'LL BE KILLED.

RETWEETS
11

FAVORITES
9

5:08 AM - 26 Sep 2014

 CEP @FightExtremism · Oct 21
.@BlackHawk21974 threatening safety of americans in Asia on @Twitter. RT & report him as spam. #CEPDigitalDisruption pic.twitter.com/IGBnlyHGpU

Abu-Sudani
@SudaniAbu

 Follow

We will March on your capitals and plant our black flags right into the heads of your leaders Insha Allah #IS #jihad #Khilafa #IslamicState

↩ Reply ♻ Retweet ★ Favorite ••• More

 CEP @FightExtremism · Oct 20
.@SudaniAbu wants to murder our leaders. RT & report him as spam. #CEPDigitalDisruption pic.twitter.com/o8YsDXZt19

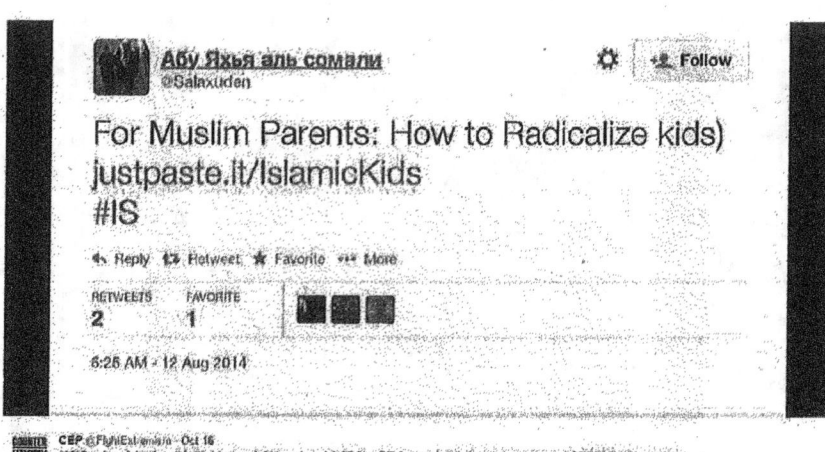

Абу Яхья аль сомали
@Salaxuden

For Muslim Parents: How to Radicalize kids)
justpaste.It/IslamicKids
#IS

↩ Reply ♺ Retweet ★ Favorite ••• More

RETWEETS   FAVORITE
2   1

6:26 AM - 12 Aug 2014

 CEP @FightExtremism · Oct 16
#ISIS extremist using @twitter to teach kids extremist ABC's. RT & report @Salaxuden as spam. #CEPDigitalDisruption
pic.twitter.com/dZiHOqJ324

Mujahid Miski
@Mujahid_Miski6   ✿   +● Follow

The necks of your citizens will be cut, so long
as you participate in the Crusade against
Islam and the Muslims. #UK #US
#AlanHennig

↩ Reply ♺ Retweet ★ Favorite ••• More

 CEP @FightExtremism · Oct 16
Hey @Twitter - #ISIS fighter @Mujahid_Miski6 is threatening to behead #Americans & Brits. #CEPDigitalDisruption pic.twitter.com/xsEqVQGWPV

State of Islam
@Dawla__account

#IS Abu Salman al-Faransi: If you can't join us you can work there in #France. Use poison in their food & drinks.

CEP @FightExtremism · Nov 28
No action from @Twitter on removing @Dawla_Account, who threatened to poison #FR citizens. #CEPDigitalDisruption pic.twitter.com/fGOpns9t9T

Ghazi
@ghazi_sham

#IS should start assaults and assassinations of ThinkTanks situated in the Middle East. They are primary centre's for collating research...

CEP @FightExtremism · Dec 2
.@ghazi_sham| & @y_dohak calling for @BrookingsInst assassinations. cc: @Charles_Lister #CEPDigitalDisruption pic.twitter.com/IzFicE35HA

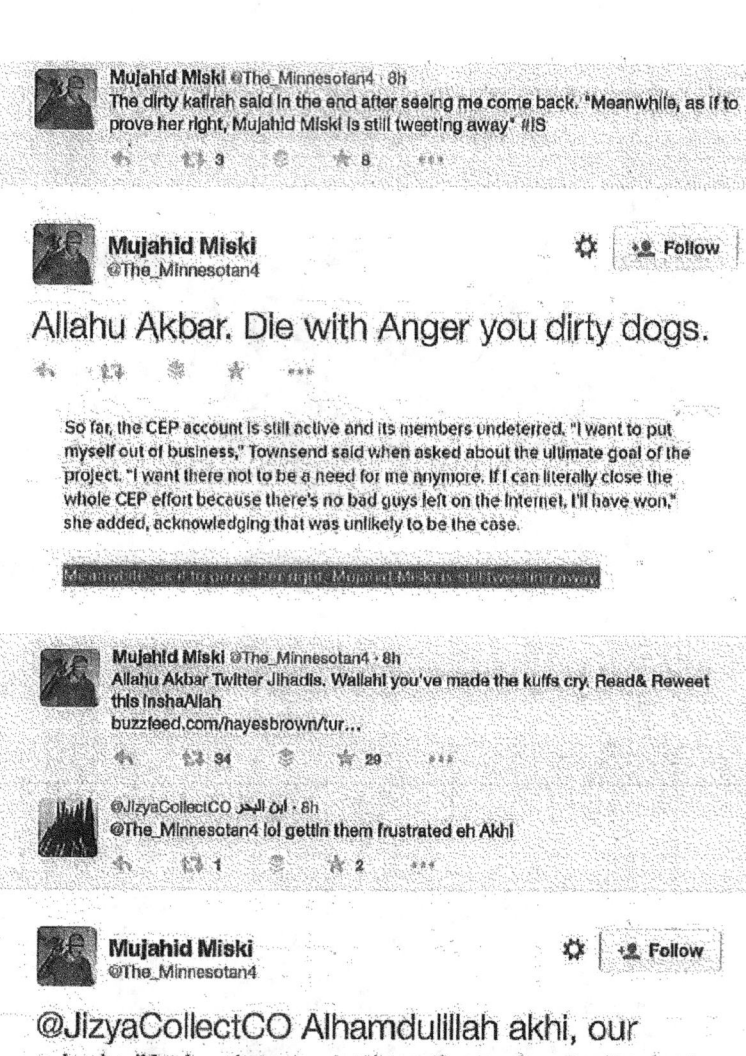

Mujahid Miski @The_Minnesotan4 · 8h
The dirty kafirah said in the end after seeing me come back. "Meanwhile, as if to prove her right, Mujahid Miski is still tweeting away" #IS

⟳ 3   ★ 8

Mujahid Miski
@The_Minnesotan4   ⚙ ＋ Follow

Allahu Akbar. Die with Anger you dirty dogs.

So far, the CEP account is still active and its members undeterred. "I want to put myself out of business," Townsend said when asked about the ultimate goal of the project. "I want there not to be a need for me anymore. If I can literally close the whole CEP effort because there's no bad guys left on the Internet, I'll have won," she added, acknowledging that was unlikely to be the case.

Meanwhile, as if to prove her right, Mujahid Miski is still tweeting away

Mujahid Miski @The_Minnesotan4 · 8h
Allahu Akbar Twitter Jihadis. Wallahi you've made the kuffs cry. Read& Reweet this InshaAllah
buzzfeed.com/hayesbrown/tur...

⟳ 34   ★ 29

@JizyaCollectCO ابن البحر · 8h
@The_Minnesotan4 lol gettin them frustrated eh Akhi

⟳ 1   ★ 2

Mujahid Miski
@The_Minnesotan4   ⚙ ＋ Follow

@JizyaCollectCO Alhamdulillah akhi, our whole life is about getting them frustrated or beheaded. #baaqiyah

FAVORITE
1

3:51 AM - 19 Nov 2014

CYBER JIHAD GATEWAY

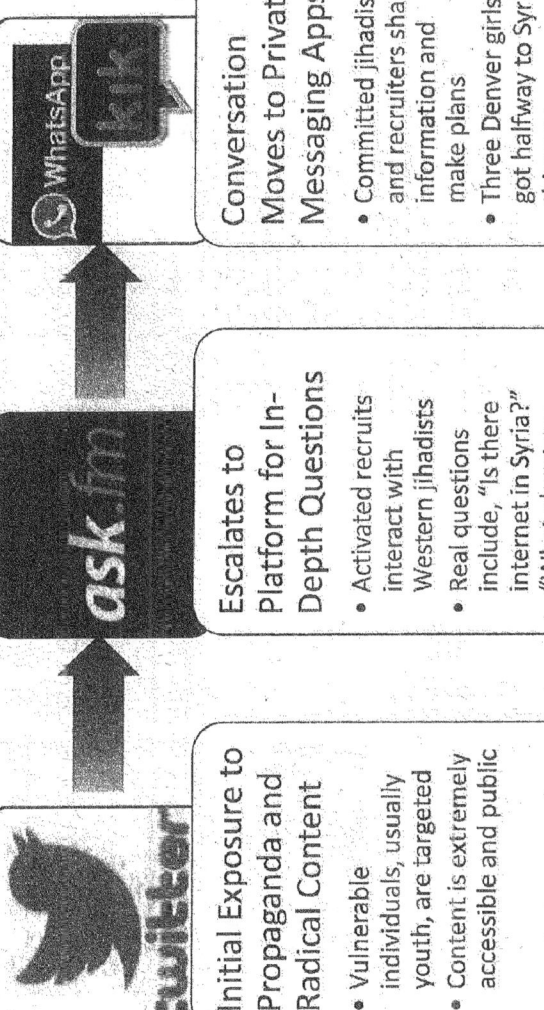

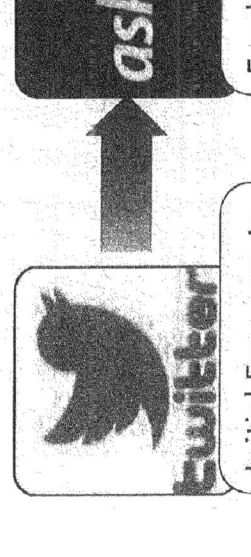

Initial Exposure to Propaganda and Radical Content

- Vulnerable individuals, usually youth, are targeted
- Content is extremely accessible and public

Escalates to Platform for In-Depth Questions

- Activated recruits interact with Western jihadists
- Real questions include, "Is there internet in Syria?" "What about my braces?"

Conversation Moves to Private Messaging Apps

- Committed jihadists and recruiters share information and make plans
- Three Denver girls got halfway to Syria this way

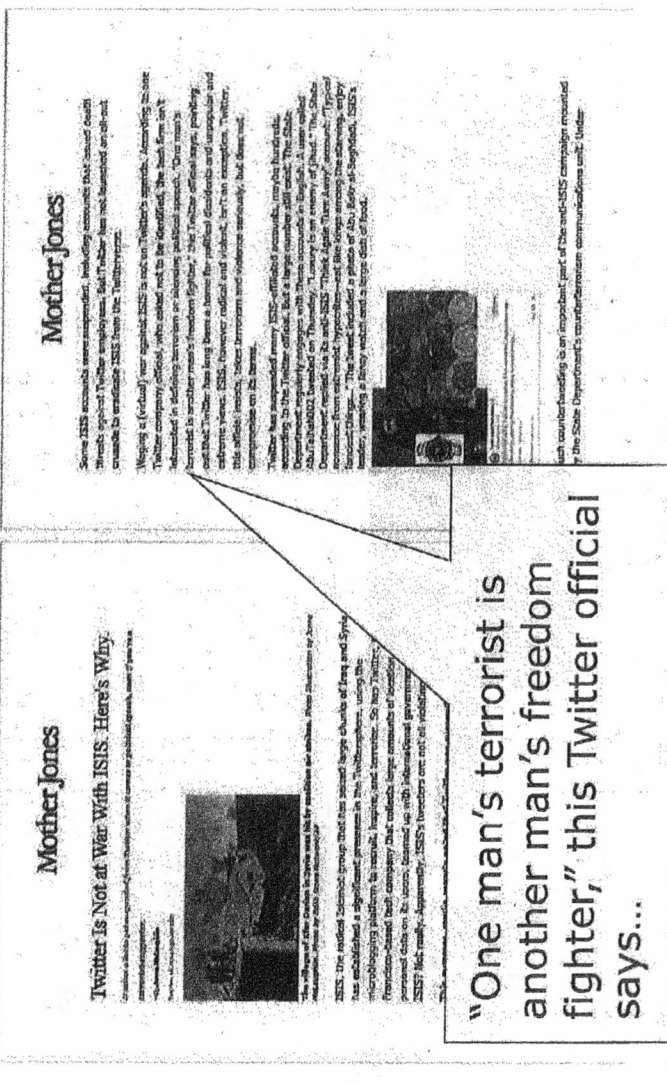

DISMISSIVE TOWARDS CONFRONTING EXTREMISM

"One man's terrorist is another man's freedom fighter," this Twitter official says....

TIMELINE OF EVENTS

OCTOBER 20, 2014
CANADA ATTACK

OCTOBER 16, 2014
REPORTS: MUJAHID MISK16

NOVEMBER 20, 2014
CEP SENDS 3RD
LETTER TO TWITTER

DECEMBER 2, 2014
MALWARE ATTACK LAUNCHED
ON CEP AND ITS FOLLOWERS

JANUARY 7, 2015
PARIS ATTACK

JANUARY 12, 2015
CENTCOM HACK

OCTOBER   NOVEMBER   DECEMBER   JANUARY

OCTOBER 27, 2014
CEP SENDS 1ST
LETTER TO TWITTER

NOVEMBER 11, 2014
CEP SENDS 2ND
LETTER TO TWITTER

NOVEMBER 21, 2014
IMAHAID MISK THREATENS
TO BEHEAD FRAN TOWNSEND

DECEMBER 15, 2014
SYDNEY SEIGE

JANUARY 27, 2015
CEP AWAITING LETTER
FROM TWITTER

OCTOBER 16, 2014
CEP DIGITAL DISRUPTION
LAUNCHED

DECEMBER 12, 2014
SHAMI WITNESS'
IDENTITY EXPOSED

JANUARY 12, 2015
CEP CALLS FOR NATIONAL
CYBER TERRORISM CENTER

COUNTER EXTREMISM PROJECT

RECOMMENDATIONS FOR SOCIAL MEDIA

1. **Trusted Reporting Status**
   - Social networks like Twitter should grant trusted reporting status to federal agencies and groups like CEP to swiftly identify and ensure the platform expeditiously bans extremists

2. **Streamlined Reporting Process**
   - Less cumbersome, more accessible reporting protocol should be added for users to report suspected violent extremist activity

3. **Clear and Open Policy on Extremism**
   - America's leading tech companies should adopt a policy statement stating that extremist activities will not be tolerated, displaying a united front in combating terrorism

4. **Verified Accounts**
   - Twitter's 'verified accounts' concept can serve as a foundation for a tiered system, whereby unverified accounts are subject to review for prohibited content

5. **Technology as the Solution**
   - There must be a technological solution, spearheaded by Silicon Valley vanguards, for security that users will accept as a tradeoff for lives saved

6. **Bright Spotlight of Transparency on Most Egregious Extremist Accounts**
   - Social media platforms should share information on the most egregious cyber-jihadis; they do not deserve anonymity for hate speech and inciting terror

COUNTER EXTREMISM PROJECT

Ambassador Mark Wallace
Chief Executive Officer
Counter Extremism Project
P.O. Box 3980
New York, NY 10185

October 27, 2014

Mr. Dick Costolo
Chief Executive Officer
Twitter
1355 Market Street, Suite 900
San Francisco, CA 94103

Dear Mr. Costolo,

We are writing on behalf of the Counter Extremism Project (CEP) – a bipartisan organization formed to combat the growing threat of extremism – to request a meeting to discuss strategies to prevent the misuse of Twitter by extremists to recruit followers, incite violence and spread hateful propaganda.

Twitter has revolutionized the way we communicate, spread knowledge, and interact with each other. Unfortunately, extremists are taking advantage of these changes by using Twitter to propagandize, self-radicalize, recruit new members and commit cyber-jihad. Extremists are hijacking and weaponizing Twitter. It is a core part of CEP's mission to stop them.

The international community has been shocked by ISIS's use of modern communication tools: the broadcast of barbaric stonings and beheadings on YouTube, the release of violent threats and intimidation against innocent civilians on AskFM and Twitter, and the Internet-wide spread and imposition of an insidious ideology that incites violence and terror. Clearly, the online communications arena is a crucial front in the comprehensive battle against ISIS.

CEP is committed to assisting in this effort. Twitter's stated policy is to remove profiles that violate Twitter terms when reported. Accordingly, CEP launched a digital campaign called #CEPDigitalDisruption to identify and highlight profiles that violate Twitter's Terms of Use policy. Our intention is to assist Twitter in eliminating ISIS profiles by exposing them.

This crowd-sourced campaign utilizes our network of CEP supporters to report each ISIS profile as spam. In the week since the launch of the #CEPDigitalDisruption a number of reports have been submitted. However, we have yet to receive a response from Twitter, and the accounts identified by CEP and its followers (along with thousands of others) remain active. Moreover, the owners of several of the ISIS fighter accounts we have exposed are working around Twitter's stated policy by changing their handles or creating new accounts.

The number of ISIS fighters misusing Twitter is growing far faster than Twitter's efforts to police and remove them. This 'defense-only' policy appears inadequate in light of the momentous challenge presented by extremists co-opting of modern communications tools such as Twitter and is allowing violent extremism to grow and fester online. We believe there is an opportunity for the Counter Extremism Project to work with Twitter to proactively identify and eliminate ISIS extremists online. The danger grows each day that goes by without a clear, bold and urgent response. We stand ready to assist and look forward to discussing possible responses with you.

We look forward to your timely response and to working together in the near future.

Sincerely,

Ambassador Mark Wallace
Chief Executive Officer
Counter Extremism Project

CC: **Vijaya Gadde**, General Counsel
        Adam Messinger, Chief Technology Officer
        Colin Crowell, Vice President, Global Public Policy
        Gabriel Stricker, Chief Communications Officer

Ambassador Mark Wallace
Chief Executive Officer

Fran Townsend
President

Counter Extremism Project
P.O. Box 3980
New York, NY 10185

November 11, 2014

Mr. Nu Wexler
Public Policy Communications, Twitter
1133 15th Street NW, 9th Floor
Washington, D.C. 20005

Dear Mr. Wexler,

We are writing on behalf of the Counter Extremism Project (CEP) to express our appreciation for your responsible decision to remove nine (9) of the violent extremist accounts that were flagged and repeatedly reported by CEP to Twitter over the past several weeks. As you know, these account holders misused Twitter as their personal vehicle for spreading messages of terror, murder and obscene acts of violence including threats of decapitation. Unfrequently, thousands of other users continue to misuse Twitter to do the same. In addition, these same individuals' aggressive recruitment of vulnerable youth has led to young people from the United States, Europe, and Australia, among others, to flock to join the likes of the Islamic State in Iraq and Syria.

Your decision to remove these accounts was the correct response to the concerns raised by CEP. However, more must be done. Comprehensive action is necessary to stop the spread of extremists' violent and threatening rhetoric through social channels like Twitter. CEP stands ready to assist in the effort. Accordingly, we are reiterating our request for a meeting with Twitter leadership to discuss strategies and options to best achieve this objective.

In addition, while Twitter's removal of certain accounts is an appropriate first step in the effort to combat extremism online, there are additional policy changes and steps to be implemented immediately that would greatly assist in halting the spread of extremism and rolling back terrorist recruitment online. For example:

**COUNTER
EXTREMISM
PROJECT**

- **Trusted Reporting Status on Twitter** – In the course of CEP's #CEPDigitalDisruption campaign, we noted that accounts reported by CEP to Twitter go into a long queue before undergoing a review. Granting CEP trusted reporting status would open a direct line of communication between CEP and Twitter enabling CEP analysis and monitors to swiftly flag extremists for removal.

- **Streamlined Reporting Process** – CEP has enlisted its supporters to report accounts to Twitter as well. These reports have also been slowed considerably by the long and cumbersome reporting process on Twitter. A new or revised reporting protocol should be added for users to report suspected terrorist/extremist activity.

- **Clear, Public Policy on Extremism** – The need for Twitter develop to a clear, public, policy statement on extremist activities is clear in light of recent developments and reports. Such a policy must clearly express the view that extremist rhetoric and other forms of misuse will not be tolerated, and that Twitter, along with partners such as CEP, will work tirelessly to identify and remove threatening and violent content. As you know, many extremists, once banned from a social network, immediately open new accounts. They often self-identify as ISIS members, jihadis and terrorists, and use similar names to their previously deactivated accounts. These extremist re-treads should be actively and swiftly identified and banned.

As expressed in our prior letter, the problem of extremist misuse of Twitter is serious and growing. In fact, Twitter was recently described in media reports as part of a 'command and control network of choice for terrorists'. Something clearly must be done.

The Counter Extremism Project looks forward to assisting Twitter in this challenging but vital endeavor. We would be happy to meet in Washington, D.C. or New York in coming two weeks. Please let us know when you are available.

Sincerely,

**Ambassador Mark Wallace
Fran Townsend**

CounterExtremism.com | P.O. Box 3980| NY, NY 10185-3980 | 212.922.0061

**COUNTER
EXTREMISM
PROJECT**

Ambassador Mark Wallace
Chief Executive Officer

Fran Townsend
President

Counter Extremism Project
P.O. Box 3980
New York, NY 10185

November 20, 2014

Mr. Dick Costolo
Chief Executive Officer
Twitter
1355 Market Street Suite 900
San Francisco, CA 94103

Dear Mr. Costolo,

We are writing on behalf of the Counter Extremism Project (CEP) to give you an update on our campaign to remove violent extremist accounts from Twitter and to ask once again for a chance to meet with you. Since we last wrote you, several more accounts have been removed, and we thank you for taking our requests seriously.

However, despite this improvement, the problem is also deepening in alarming terms. Many of the extremists you have suspended continue to resurface within a few hours with a new account, gloating about how they cannot and will not be beaten.

We are particularly concerned with Mujahid Miski, who has now gone so far as to use Twitter to threaten the beheading of our President, Fran Townsend, a former White House official.

An American citizen, Miski left his home state of Minnesota at the age of 18 to join the extremist movement in Somalia. He is an ardent ISIS sympathizer and recruiter, and has a wide network of Twitter followers and supporters. He has been and remains a high priority US government counter terrorism target because he is a serious and credible national security threat.

Miski is currently on his eleventh Twitter account, using the handle @Abu_Jannah11. He has been suspended multiple times and has avoided suspension in the past by changing his Twitter handle. In this current incarnation, his rhetoric is as violent and aggressive as ever, but this time his threats are hitting close to home. After the recent attack in Jerusalem, Miski

COUNTER EXTREMISM PROJECT

celebrated, calling the perpetrators "brave" and saying that every Muslim should kill at least one Jew.

Since the BuzzFeed article where we initially expressed our frustration with the Twitter reporting process, Miski has been making implied threats towards Fran Townsend, the President of our organization. We have included these threatening tweets on the following page. He continues to incite violence and extremism daily – if not hourly – and will continue to do so if further action is not taken.

We have reported Miski's threats to Townsend to the FBI. For now, our hands are tied as law enforcement takes over.

But the hands of Twitter's leaders are not. We are again asking you to take a deeper look at your policy regarding reporting violent and extremist tweets, to give CEP trusted reporting status and to streamline the reporting process overall. We understand that this cannot be accomplished overnight, but we are more than willing to be a part of the process and work with Twitter.

CEP is ready to meet with Twitter in Washington, D.C. or New York City in the coming weeks. Please let us know when you are available.

Sincerely,

Ambassador Mark Wallace
Fran Townsend

COUNTER EXTREMISM PROJECT

Mujahid Miski @The_Minnesotan4 · 8h
The dirty kafirah said in the end after seeing me come back, "Meanwhile, as if to prove her right, Mujahid Miski is still tweeting away" //IS

⭐ ⇄ 3   ⭐   ⭐ 8   •••

Mujahid Miski
@The_Minnesotan4

⚙ ⚫ Follow

Allahu Akbar. Die with Anger you dirty dogs.

⤺   ⇄   ✎   ☆   •••

So far, the CEP account is still active and its members undeterred. "I want to put myself out of business," Townsend said when asked about the ultimate goal of the project. "I want there not to be a need for me anymore. If I can literally close the whole CEP effort because there's no bad guys left on the Internet, I'll have won," she added, acknowledging that was unlikely to be the case.

COUNTER EXTREMISM PROJECT

Mujahid Miski @The_Minnesotan4 · 8h
Allahu Akbar Twitter Jihadis. Wallahi you've made the kuffs cry. Read & Retweet this InshaAllah
buzzfeed.com/hayesbrown/tur...
94   29

@JizyaCollectCO البحر ou · 8h
@The_Minnesotan4 lol gettin them frustrated eh Akhi.
1   2

Mujahid Miski
@The_Minnesotan4   ⚙ 👤 Follow

@JizyaCollectCO Alhamdulillah akhi, our whole life is about getting them frustrated or beheaded. #baaqiyah

FAVORITE
1

3:51 AM · 19 Nov 2014

COUNTER EXTREMISM PROJECT

RESPONSE FROM TWITTER, DATED OCTOBER 31, 2014:

Dan,

Thanks for your message. Below is some information about our policies that address the issues raised in your letter.

- We have 284 million users worldwide sending approximately 500 million Tweets per day, and we do not proactively monitor content on the platform.
- Our rules outline content and conduct boundaries, including a ban on direct violent threats.
- Users report potential rules violations to us, we review them, and take action when appropriate.
- Our Guidelines for Law Enforcement explain what information we have about accounts, and how authorities can request it.
- Our most recent transperency report showed over 2,000 government requests during the first half of this year, including 1,200 from the United States.

Please let me know if we can get acditional information for you.

Best,

Nu

Nu Wexler | Twitter, Inc. | Public Policy Communications | Washington, DC |

Mr. POE. The Chair will next recognize Mr. Berger for his 5-minute testimony.

STATEMENT OF MR. J.M. BERGER, AUTHOR

Mr. BERGER. Thank you, Mr. Chairman, and thank you, members of the committee.

I want to talk a little bit about the scope of the problem and sort of try and put some hard numbers on what we are talking about here because a lot of the discussion we have about this is often very general and on principle—we know it is bad but we don't know exactly what it is.

We are going to focus on Twitter partly because it is easier to do this kind of analysis on Twitter and also, as the chairman noted and as Ambassador Wallace noted, Twitter has a particular problem with this that it is in the process of adjusting its approach to, as opposed to Facebook and YouTube who have made changes over the last couple of years.

So in a forthcoming study on ISIS' use of Twitter, which was commissioned by Google Ideas and will be published by the Brookings Institution's project on U.S. relations with the Islamist world, technologist Jonathan Morgan and I set out to develop metrics that could define the size and function of the Islamic State's presence on Twitter.

While our analysis is not complete, we can confidently estimate that throughout last fall at least 45,000 Twitter accounts were used by ISIS supporters. This figure includes accounts that were both created and suspended during the time it took us to collect the data.

The size of the network has certainly changed since this estimate but it remains only a minuscule fraction of the overall Twitter user base. Our research began at the same time that Twitter started an aggressive campaign of suspending accounts so it reflects some of the effects of those suspensions.

What it doesn't do is give us a baseline to look at to see what the environment without suspensions is, which is unfortunate, but the timing dictated that.

Almost three-quarters of ISIS supporters on Twitter that we studied had fewer than 500 followers each. Only a handful had more than 20,000.

Suspended users—people we were able to determine definitively had been suspended as opposed to changing their name or deleting their own account—had generally tweeted three times as often as those who were not suspended, and received almost 10 times as many retweets from other ISIS supporters.

Suspended users averaged twice as many followers as those who were not suspended. When users are removed from the system, when they are suspended or they delete themselves or for whatever reason they stop taking part, we did see some evidence that the existing accounts compensate.

So other people step up or new accounts are created. The accounts that already exist increase their activity. But the preliminary evidence suggests that they can't fully regenerate the network if suspensions continue at a consistent pace.

One big part of this debate, you know, has been this Whac-A-Mole concept. It is, like, you know, does it help to delete these accounts, does it help to suspend these people? And I think that so far what we are seeing is there is pretty good evidence that it does limit what they can do online.

We confirmed at least 800 ISIS supporters suspensions between last fall and this month's and there are indications there were thousands more that we could not confirm, possibly well over 10,000 more.

While tens of thousands of accounts remain, ISIS supporters online called the effects of these suspensions devastating. There are three important benefits to the current level of suspension.

First, they reduce ISIS' reach among users at risk of radicalization. People don't spring from the womb fully radicalized. They have to find a path to radicalization, to talk to a recruiter, to get information about the movement. Suspensions don't eliminate that path but they increase the cost of participation.

Second, while ISIS' reach has been reduced, enough accounts remain to provide an important open source intelligence. So that is the other piece of this debate, you know, is there valuable intelligence that we are losing out on when we suspend these guys.

And, you know, if you have 30,000 or 40,000 accounts that are all very limited reach, you can get a lot of intelligence from that without necessarily allowing them to operate unfettered.

Third, the targeting of the most active members of the ISIS supporter network, which is what is currently happening in terms of the Twitter suspensions we have seen, undercuts ISIS' most important strategic advantage on this platform, which is about 2,000 to 3,000 supporter accounts that are much more active than ordinary Twitter users.

This is an explicit strategy of ISIS. They put out documents about it. They have a name for the group—they call them the mujahideen, which is Arabic for industrious—and they are the people who drive this activity.

The reason we are talking about this now is that these over achievers who get online and are extremely active are able to drive a lot more traffic. They are able to cause ISIS hashtags to trend and get aggregated by third parties.

They are able to influence search results. So if somebody is searching for information on Baghdad they might get an ISIS threat instead of whatever information they were trying to seek.

So what we see right now is that there is a lot of pressure on this network and I think that there is a balance that we are pretty close to achieving. But there is definitely room for improvement.

[The prepared statement of Mr. Berger follows:]

J.M. Berger
Nonresident fellow, the Brookings Institution
House Committee on Foreign Affairs
"The Evolution of Terrorist Propaganda: The Paris Attack and Social Media"
January 27. 2015

Terrorist use of technology can be complex, but it is not mysterious. Extremists generally follow the same practices available to everyone, from dial-up bulletin boards in the 1990s to social media today.

Jihadists have figured out how to use social media to make an impact, even though their numbers are miniscule in comparison to the overall user base, with Islamic State, more commonly known as ISIS or ISIL, leads the way. Its highly organized social media campaign uses deceptive tactics and shows a sophisticated understanding of how such networks operate.

After years of back and forth debate among free speech advocates, government and companies, Facebook and YouTube have instituted reporting procedures that allow users to flag content that supports terrorism for removal.

Until last fall, Twitter took an extremely permissive approach to the question of what content it would permit. Starting shortly before ISIS disseminated a video of the beheading of American journalist James Foley, Twitter began to take a more aggressive approach to ISIS specifically, and thousands of ISIS supporter accounts have been suspended since. Other jihadist groups have been targeted, but in lesser numbers.

In a forthcoming study on ISIS's use of Twitter, commissioned by Google Ideas and to be published by the Brookings Institution's Project on U.S. Relations with the Islamic World, technologist Jonathon Morgan and I set out to develop metrics that could define the size and function of this coordinated effort on Twitter.

While our analysis is not complete, we can confidently estimate that during the autumn of 2014, there were at least 45,000 Twitter accounts used by ISIS supporters. This figure includes accounts that were both created and suspended during the time it took us to collect the data.

Our full findings will be published in March and may reflect a higher estimate for the autumn 2014 time frame. The current size of the network has likely changed and is possibly smaller, but we are still collecting data for that assessment.

Our research began at the same time that Twitter started an aggressive campaign to suspend ISIS supporter accounts, so it reflects some of the effects of suspensions.

We found that the vast majority of ISIS supporters on Twitter, about 73 percent, had fewer than 500 followers each. During that period of time, we found no accounts actively supporting ISIS that possessed more than 50,000 followers, a sharp change from early 2014 when some ISIS users could be found with more than 80,000 followers.

The pace of activity – the number of tweets per day – was perhaps the important factor in determining who would be suspended. Suspended users tweeted three times as often as those who were not suspended, and received almost 10 times as many retweets from other ISIS supporters. Suspended users averaged twice as many followers as those who were not suspended.

When users are removed from the system, we found evidence that existing users do compensate to some extent, but preliminary evidence suggests they cannot fully regenerate the network if the suspensions continue at a consistent pace.

We noted that almost 800 confirmed ISIS supporter accounts were suspended between fall 2014 and January 2015. This may be the tip of the iceberg, as we also identified almost 18,000 accounts related to the ISIS network which were suspended during the same time frame. We were not able to estimate how many of the 18,000 were ISIS supporters, but we suspect it is a significant number.

ISIS supporters on Twitter are under significant pressure, with the most active and viral users taking the brunt of the suspensions. While tens of thousands remain, ISIS supporters online call the effects of these suspensions "devastating."

There are three important benefits to the current level of suspensions.

First, they reduce ISIS's reach among online populations at risk of radicalization. ISIS supporters do not spring from the womb fully radicalized, and a path is required between recruiters and the vulnerable. Suspensions do not eliminate that path, but they create obstacles and increase the cost of participation.

Second, by allowing some ISIS accounts to continue with a lower profile, the current level of suspension activity preserves a substantial amount of open-source intelligence.

Third, targeting the most active members of the ISIS supporter network undercuts ISIS's most important strategic advantage on platforms like Twitter – the 1,000 to 3,000 accounts that are, at any given time, far more active than ordinary Twitter users.

These accounts – described fully in data collected over the last two years as well as in ISIS strategy documents – act in a coordinated way to amplify ISIS's message, tweeting links to ISIS propaganda and hashtags at an unnaturally fast pace, which causes them place higher in search results and results in content being aggregated by third parties. The workings of this system will be described in substantial detail in the forthcoming book, "ISIS: The State of Terror," by Jessica Stern and J.M. Berger.

In addition, ISIS and more recently, al Qaeda in the Arabian Peninsula, use "bots," computer-controlled Twitter accounts that automatically send out content in a similar manner. Thousands of such bots support ISIS and other illegal ventures.

The suspensions also make ISIS vulnerable to its own tactics. For instance, ISIS critics in the Persian Gulf have recently taken to paying spammers to send out thousands of tweets criticizing ISIS, often at a higher volume than ISIS supporters.

In conclusion, I believe the current environment is approaching the right balance of pressure on ISIS networks, degrading its ability to achieve its goals while still allowing the United States to exploit open source intelligence from the network of members and supporters online.

That said, we can do better in three areas.

First, transparency. All stakeholders need to clearly understand exactly why and how a user gets suspended on social media. Companies need to communicate this better.

Second, consistency. If suspensions do not continue at a consistent pace and with consistent criteria, the targeted network will regenerate. The suspension process is akin to weeding a garden. You don't "defeat" weeds, you manage them, and if you stop weeding, they will grow back.

Third, scope. ISIS far from our only problem on social media. Aside from other terrorists who are already taking lessons from the Islamic State's tactics, challenges on social media range from bullying and targeted harassment to extensive activities by foreign state-sponsored disinformation and intelligence programs.

Finally, it is important to note that no single authority exists for dealing with these issues. The concerns of corporations are different from those of governments and those of activists, and the concerns of governments and activists are wildly different around the globe.

Any approach to social media policing needs to include some consideration of our multipolar world. In our fight against terrorism, we do not wish to create precedents and authorities that would empower tyrants and repressive movements with tools to silence legitimate dissent.

———————

Mr. POE. The gentleman yields back his time.

The Chair now recognizes Mr. Kohlmann for his 5-minute opening statement. Mr. Kohlmann?

STATEMENT OF MR. EVAN KOHLMANN, CHIEF INFORMATION OFFICER, FLASHPOINT PARTNERS

Mr. KOHLMANN. Thank you, Mr. Chairman. Thank you, members of the committee.

As more young people from the U.S. and other Western countries seek to depart to join jihadi front lines abroad, there has been an increasing public awareness of the role that online social media is serving and recruiting them to the cause.

Yet, recently there has been a noticeable divergence from traditional jihadi chat forums to the slicker interfaces and enormous global audience that has been afforded by services like Facebook and Twitter.

Indeed, the trend toward jihadists exploiting Western commercial social media platforms has been in full view in the aftermath of this month's terrorist attacks in Paris.

Through relatively little is known about how the Kouachi brothers and Amedy Coulibaly were using social media, claims of responsibility for the attacks in Paris emerged quite quickly from al-Qaeda in the Arabian Peninsula, AQAP, all of which were distributed exclusively via Twitter.

On January 9, AQAP's media wing used its account on Twitter to disseminate download links for a message from its official, Hareth al-Nadhari, praising the Paris attacks and lamenting only that, "I wish I had been there with you."

On January 14, again, using the exact same Twitter account, AQAP distributed download links for a direct video recorded claim of responsibility for the Paris attacks from senior official, Nasr al-Ansi, in which he declared, "The one who chose the target, laid the plan and financed the operation is the leadership of this organization."

In fact, as of right now, AQAP, which is a designated terrorist organization under U.S. law, has not one but two official accounts on Twitter: One for releasing videos and one for releasing breaking news updates.

Nor is AQAP alone. Other allied factions such as al-Qaeda and the Islamic Maghreb have also begun to eschew the traditional route of publishing media on these forums and instead are releasing material directly on Twitter.

Over the past 3 months, AQAP's public Twitter account has only been disabled by administrators on four occasions. Each time it has been disabled, AQAP has merely created a new account with the same name appended with 1, 2, 3, 4, respectively. There is not much mystery in which Twitter account AQAP will register next unless you have trouble counting to five.

Nonetheless, Twitter is not the only offender here and this leads to another aspect of jihadi social media that surfaced as a result of Paris and that is the Internet video that featured Amedy Coulibaly claiming responsibility for the attacks in the name of ISIS.

In the video, Coulibaly condemned recent Western air strikes on ISIS and threatened, "If you attack the Caliphate, if you attack the Islamic State, we will attack you."

Links to this video were first posted on ISIS' main online chat forum, alplatformmedia.com and, naturally, the question that follows from this analysis is: How is ISIS able to operate its own official .com social media platform on the Internet in order to disseminate its media?

And the answer to that question is another billion-dollar San Francisco-based company called CloudFlare, which aims to shield Web sites from being targeted by spammers, cyber criminals and denial of service attacks.

CloudFlare in essence serves as a gatekeeper to control the flow of unwanted visitors to a given site. It has advanced detection features that thwart attempts by automated robots to scrape data from and monitor these forums.

In fact, two of ISIS' top three online chat forums, including alplatformmedia.com, are currently guarded by CloudFlare.

Without such protection, these sites would almost certainly succumb to the same relentless online attacks that have completely collapsed several major jihadi web forums in recent years.

In 2013, after CloudFlare was accused of providing protection to terrorist Web sites, the company CEO insisted that,

> "It would not be right for us to monitor the content that flows through our network and make determinations on what is and what is not politically appropriate. Frankly, that would be creepy."

He also asserted,

> "A Web site is speech. It is not a bomb. There is no imminent danger it creates and no provider has an affirmative obligation to monitor and make determinations about the theoretically harmful nature of speech a site may contain."

It is extremely difficult to reconcile the logical paradox that it is currently illegal under U.S. law to give pro bono assistance to a terrorist group in order to convince them to adopt politics instead of violence but it is perfectly legal for CloudFlare to commercially profit from a terrorist group by assisting them to disseminate propaganda which encourages mass murder.

In fact, CloudFlare's CEO has been adamant that, "CloudFlare abides by all applicable laws in the countries in which we operate and we firmly support the due process of law."

The multi-billion-dollar U.S. companies who provide social media services to ISIS and al-Qaeda are well aware that the way American law is presently structured it is almost impossible for them to ever be held responsible for the mayhem that their paying users might cause.

The only real incentive they have to address this problem is when it becomes so glaring, as it was in the case of James Foley, that they are briefly forced to take action to save public face.

Permitting U.S. commercial interests to simply ignore vital national security concerns and earn profits from consciously providing high-tech services to terrorist organizations is not an acceptable legal framework in the 21st century.

Thank you very much.

[The prepared statement of Mr. Kohlmann follows:]

Testimony of

Evan F. Kohlmann

with Laith Alkhouri and Alexandra Kassirer

Before the

House Committee on Foreign Affairs
Subcommittee on Terrorism, Nonproliferation, and Trade

"The Evolution of Terrorist Propaganda: The Paris Attack and Social Media"

Charlie Hebdo and the Jihadi Online Network: Assessing the Role of American Commercial Social Media Platforms

January 27, 2015; 2:30pm

2172 Rayburn House Office Building

Washington D.C.

Evan F. Kohlmann
Co-Founder - Chief Innovation Officer
Flashpoint Global Partners; New York, NY
www.flashpoint-intel.com - info@flashpoint-intel.com
Voicemail/Fax: (206)202-4911

EVAN F. KOHLMANN
A Biographical Sketch

Evan Kohlmann is a co-founder of Flashpoint Global Partners, a New York-based "dark web" data mining and security consulting firm, and is responsible for innovation and product development. He has served as a private sector International Terrorism Consultant who has spent more than a decade tracking Al-Qaida and other terrorist organizations by studying their digital and online communications. Mr. Kohlmann has testified over thirty times as an expert witness in U.S. federal courts, and has served at various times as a contract consultant in terrorism matters on behalf of the U.S. Department of Defense, the U.S. Department of Justice, the Federal Bureau of Investigation (FBI), the Office of the High Representative (OHR) in Bosnia-Herzegovina, the International Criminal Tribunal for the Former Yugoslavia (ICTFY) at the Hague, the Australian Federal Police (AFP), the U.K. Crown Prosecution Service (CPS), Scotland Yard's SO-15 Counter Terrorism Command, the Central Scotland Police, West Yorkshire Police, the Danish Security and Intelligence Service (PET), and the Swiss Federal Prosecutor's Office. Mr. Kohlmann also currently serves as an on-air analyst on behalf of NBC News / MSNBC.

Mr. Kohlmann holds an undergraduate degree in International Politics from the Edmund A. Walsh School of Foreign Service (Georgetown University), and a graduate degree in law from the University of Pennsylvania Law School. Kohlmann is also the recipient of a certificate in Islamic studies from the Prince Alwaleed bin Talal Center for Muslim-Christian Understanding (CMCU) at Georgetown University.

As more young people from the United States and other Western countries—who have no prior links to Syria or the jihadi organizations fighting there—seek to depart to join the frontline in the Levant, there has been an increasing public awareness of the role that jihadi online social media and networks are serving in recruiting them to the cause and providing them with the basic guidance necessary to reach their destination. This has come both in the form of indirect recruitment (i.e. glossy English-language propaganda videos and magazines distributed on the Internet), as well as direct recruitment by Western jihadists in Syria and Iraq who have regular access to major commercial social media platforms like YouTube, Facebook, Twitter, Skype, Tumblr, and Kik. Several weeks ago, Zarine Khan—the mother of a 19-year-old Illinois man facing federal charges for attempting to travel to Syria—emotionally addressed a news conference and denounced "the brainwashing and recruiting of children through the use of social media and the Internet... We have a message for ISIS, Mr. Baghdadi and his fellow social-media recruiters: Leave our children alone!"[1]

The influx of Americans and other social-media-savvy Westerners seems to have bred a noticeable divergence from traditional proprietary Arabic-language jihadi chat forums to the slicker interfaces and enormous global audience afforded by services like Facebook and Twitter. The odd sense of comfort that Western jihadists fighting in Syria and Iraq feel in using such platforms is somewhat disturbing. After engaging in live discussion for several hours last October via the Kik Messenger service with Farah Shirdon, a Somali-Canadian ISIS fighter in Mosul, he told me, "for the next week I'll be busy going to Syria to handle some[thing] so we need to finish this up tomorrow." Young millenials like Mr. Shirdon are so confident in the reliability and security of these big name social media companies that they have not even a second thought about disclosing such potentially sensitive information—even to known adversaries.

The trend towards jihadists exploiting (and indeed relying upon) Western commercial social media platforms for their online communications has been in full view in the aftermath of this month's terrorist attacks in Paris. Though relatively little is known about how the Kouachi brothers and Amedy Coulibaly were using social media prior to the attacks, claims of responsibility for the tragic events in Paris emerged quite quickly from Al-Qaida in the Arabian Peninsula (AQAP)—all of which were distributed exclusively via Twitter. On January 9, an account purportedly run by a fighter in the ranks of AQAP, "Bakhsarouf Al-Yemen," tweeted that AQAP was behind the attack and promised his followers that an official claim of credit would soon be released, but that it had been delayed due to "security reasons."[2] The Twitter user directly addressed "the relationship between Al-Qaida and the Charlie Hebdo battle: the relationship is direct and the operation was supervised by Al-Qaida's branch in the Arabian Peninsula. The operation was directed by the leadership of AQAP, and they chose these targets carefully, to avenge the honor of our prophet... and in France specifically, for its role that is not hidden in the war on Islam."[3]

Later on the same day, AQAP's official Al-Malahem media wing used its account on Twitter to disseminate download links for an audio message of AQAP official Hareth

---

[1] Tarm, Michael. "Mother of Chicago teen to Islamic State: 'Leave our children alone!'" Associated Press. January 13, 2015.

[2] https://twitter.com/ba_yman/status/553652768628813825

[3] https://twitter.com/ba_yman/status/553652768628813825

al-Nadhari praising the Paris attacks and condemning France: "men from among the faithful soldiers of Allah embarked and taught them how to be polite and the limits on freedom of expression; soldiers came to you who love Allah and his messenger, who do not care about death, and who are fond of martyrdom for the cause of Allah... O' heroic mujahideen... may your hands be preserved... I wish I was there with you."[4] On January 14, again using the same Twitter account, AQAP distributed download links for a direct claim of responsibility for the Paris attacks in the form of a video from senior AQAP leader Nasr bin Ali al-Ansi.[5] In the video, al-Ansi declared that AQAP engineered the attacks "as a vengeance for the Messenger of Allah. We clarify to the ummah that the one who chose the target, laid the plan and financed the operation, is the leadership of the organization." Al-Ansi further mocked the unity rallies that took place in Paris in the wake of the attacks: "Look at how they gathered, rallied and supported each other; strengthening their weakness and dressing their wounds. Those wounds have not healed and they won't, be it in Paris, New York or Washington, or in London or Spain."[6]

In fact, as of the time of this testimony, AQAP—a designated foreign terrorist organization according to U.S. law—has not one, but two official accounts on Twitter— one for releasing videos and recordings and the other for releasing statements and breaking news updates. Nor is AQAP alone—other allied factions such as Al-Qaida in the Islamic Maghreb (AQIM) have also begun to eschew the traditional established route of publishing jihadi media through password-protected proprietary jihadi chat forums and instead they have been releasing material directly via Twitter. This process has taken place quite seamlessly despite reported initiatives by Twitter to curb the use of its network for terrorist propaganda in the wake of the recorded beheadings of James Foley and other Western journalists captured in Syria. Over the past three months, AQAP's public Twitter account has only been disabled by system administrators on four occasions. Each time it has been disabled, AQAP has merely created a new account with the same name, appended with "1", "2", "3", and "4" respectively. Thus, there is hardly any mystery in what Twitter account AQAP will register next.

The failure of Twitter to learn from and adapt to this rudimentary pattern would suggest fundamental failures in its responsibility to prevent its service from becoming a mouthpiece for terrorist organizations. One jihadist has smugly advised Twitter to simply sit back and "let us continue spread our daawah (JIHAD)" because the company's current efforts aimed at thwarting such uses are pointless: "it takes 2 minutes to get new acc[ounts]."[7] It should be emphasized that AQAP's videos and statements about the Paris attacks have only been released on Twitter, and—weeks later—still have yet to appear in the areas of elite Arabic-language jihadi chat forums that are reserved for the group. This means that Twitter is not only their preferred means of propaganda distribution, it is verging on being their sole one as well. While Twitter's CEO Dick Costolo has insisted that Twitter is "actively suspending accounts as we discover them", the company also acknowledges that some offending accounts are nonetheless left online

---

[4] https://twitter.com/AMOJAH3/status/553666443355910144
[5] https://twitter.com/amojah3/status/555305155437268992
[6] https://twitter.com/amojah3/status/555305155437268992
[7] https://twitter.com/Abuhaitham12/status/559324286314618880

by system administrators due to "public interest factors such as the newsworthiness of the content."[8]

Nonetheless, Twitter is not the only offender here. The primarily text-based communication service may be ideal for rapidly distributing download links, but not broadcasting the video files themselves. The actual AQAP audio and video content addressing the Paris attacks are hosted on services that include Google's YouTube streaming service; Shenandoah, Texas-based cloud storage company Mediafire.com; and the San Francisco-based 501(c)(3) non-profit Internet Archive (www.archive.org). While YouTube and Mediafire.com have become somewhat more adept at disabling terrorist propaganda hosted on their networks, the Internet Archive has become the de-facto preferred storage point for jihadi audio and videos, whether from AQAP or ISIS. Archive.org was founded in 1996 with the noble intent of building an Internet library and providing "permanent access" to "historical collections that exist in digital format."[9] Unfortunately, in the present era, the term "historical collections" is now broad enough to encompass jihadist propaganda in the form of graphic beheading and execution videos, suicide bombings, and claims of responsibility for the attacks in Paris—which have been permanently preserved on Archive.org in their original, high-resolution formats. The fact that this powerful propaganda remains easily accessible raises the question of when the principles of open reporting and freedom of speech can or should be extended to include incitement to racial and ethnic hate, and calls for violence from terrorist organizations.

This leads to another aspect of jihadi social media that surfaced as a result of the Paris attacks: the apparently conflicting video released on January 10 that featured Amedy Coulibaly claiming responsibility for the attacks in the name of ISIS. In the video, Coulibaly condemned recent Western airstrikes on ISIS and insisted, "You act like the victims as if you don't understand what's been happening for months... If you attack the Caliphate, if you attack the Islamic State, we will attack you. You can't attack and not expect a response."[10] He also explained the nature of his relationship with the Kouachi brothers: "Brothers in our team divided themselves in two... We worked partly together, but also partly separate, it's more like a pact." Links to the Coulibaly video were first posted in a general discussion room of the main ISIS online chat forum Alplatformmedia.com by an ordinary registered user "Amir Monsaf"—and not by an authorized courier from ISIS' official media wing.[11] After the content of the video became clear, the message containing the download links was moved by forum administrators to the official ISIS media room. This sequence of events, and the lack of any watermark on the video from an official ISIS media unit, strongly suggests that it was produced and distributed by unknown parties independent of ISIS. As with the AQAP videos, the video of Mr. Coulibaly itself was hosted on YouTube, the Internet Archive, and several other U.S.-based cloud hosting services.

The natural question that follows from this analysis is how does ISIS manage to reliably operate its own official proprietary dot-com social media platform on the Internet in order to disseminate videos such as the beheading of James Foley and the

---

[8] Parkinson, Hannah Jane. "James Foley: How social media is fighting back against Isis propaganda." Guardian (London). August 20, 2014.
[9] https://archive.org/about/
[10] http://www.alplatformmedia.com/vb/showthread.php?t=77118.
[11] http://www.alplatformmedia.com/vb/showthread.php?t=77118.

"martyrdom" will of Amedy Coulibaly? The answer is another San Francisco-based American tech security company called CloudFlare, which aims to shield Internet websites and resources from being targeted by spammers, cybercriminals, and frustrating denial-of-service attacks. CloudFlare, which boasts that 4% of all web requests flows through its network, in essence serves as gatekeeper to control the flow of visitors to given sites and to verify that those visitors have a legitimate purpose in visiting them.[12] It has advanced detection features that complicate (or thwart entirely) attempts by automated robots to scrape data from and monitor these forums, including browser tests and so-called "captcha codes." In fact, two of ISIS' top three online chat forums—including the notorious Alplatformmedia.com—are currently guarded by CloudFlare. Without such protection from CloudFlare, these sites would almost certainly succumb to the same relentless online attacks that have completely collapsed several major jihadi web forums over the past two years.

In 2013, after CloudFlare was contacted by journalists over allegations that their service was providing protection to terrorist websites, the company's CEO Matthew Prince published a full explanation of their policy in this regard. According to Prince, it would not "be right for us to monitor the content that flows through our network and make determinations on what is and what is not politically appropriate. Frankly, that would be creepy... Removing this, or any other site, from our network wouldn't remove the content from the Internet: it would simply slow its performance and make it more vulnerable to attack."[13] In his response, Prince also asserted:

> "A website is speech. It is not a bomb. There is no imminent danger it creates and no provider has an affirmative obligation to monitor and make determinations about the theoretically harmful nature of speech a site may contain... There are lots of things on the web I find personally distasteful. I have political beliefs, but I don't believe those beliefs should color what is and is not allowed to flow over the network. As we have blogged about before, we often find ourselves on opposite sides of political conflicts. Fundamentally, we are consistent in the fact that our political beliefs will not color who we allow to be fast and safe on the web."[14]

In June 2010, in the context of the case of <u>Holder v. Humanitarian Law Project</u>, the U.S. Supreme Court upheld a strict view of the "expert advice and assistance" clause of U.S. counterterrorism laws, making even nonviolent advocacy potentially an illicit form of material support if it is carried out in conjunction with a proscribed terrorist organization.[15] The case had specifically centered on a group of American civil rights activists who advertised their mission as helping such groups "find peaceful ways to achieve [their] goals." It is extremely difficult to reconcile the logical paradox that it is currently illegal to give pro-bono assistance to a terrorist group in order for them to adopt politics instead of violence, but it is perfectly legal for CloudFlare to commercially profit from a terrorist group by assisting them to communicate securely with recruits and to publicly disseminate recordings of mass murder. Indeed, CloudFlare CEO Matthew

---

[12] https://blog.cloudflare.com/cloudflare-and-free-speech/

[13] https://blog.cloudflare.com/cloudflare-and-free-speech/

[14] https://blog.cloudflare.com/cloudflare-and-free-speech/

[15] Liptak, Adam. "Court Affirms Ban on Aiding Groups Tied to Terror." New York Times. June 21, 2010.

Prince has been adamant in his declarations that "CloudFlare abides by all applicable laws in the countries in which we operate and we firmly support the due process of law."[16] Prince continues to insist, "We have never received a request to terminate the site in question from any law enforcement authority, let alone a valid order from a court."[17]

In deference to CloudFlare, it is possible that the company has received a formal request from law enforcement to continue providing its services to such an illicit online forum. Yet, even as one who has repeatedly advocated leaving jihadi forums online in order to study those who use them, this possibility gives me pause for reflection. If so, there must be a careful assessment of the potential negative policy impacts of leaving ISIS recruitment platforms online and unmolested in light of the recognition that Western security services are abjectly failing to track, identify, and stop all of those who are using these sites.

The multi-billion dollar U.S. companies who provide social media services to ISIS and Al-Qaida are well aware that the way American law is presently structured, it is almost impossible for them to ever be held legally liable or responsible for the potential mayhem that their paying users might cause. The only real incentive they have to address this problem is when it becomes so glaring and embarrassing, as it was in the case of slain American journalist James Foley, that they are temporarily forced to take action to save public face. Without concerted pressure both from the American people as well as the Congress—in addition to meaningful legal reform aimed at closing loopholes that allow service providers to turn a blind eye to the identities of their users—this problem is almost certain to grow steadily worse in the months and years to come. Permitting U.S. commercial interests to simply ignore vital national security concerns and earn profits from consciously providing high-tech services to banned terrorist organizations is not an acceptable legal framework in the 21st century.

---

[16] https://blog.cloudflare.com/cloudflare-and-free-speech/
[17] https://blog.cloudflare.com/cloudflare-and-free-speech/

Mr. POE. I thank the gentleman.

Now we will hear from our final witness, Ms. MacKinnon, for your 5-minute opening statement.

STATEMENT OF MS. REBECCA MACKINNON, DIRECTOR, RANKING DIGITAL RIGHTS, NEW AMERICA

Ms. MACKINNON. Thank you very much, Mr. Chairman, Ranking Member Keating, members of the committee.

So how do we fight terrorism and violent extremism, which are obvious problems as we have just been hearing, in the Internet age while not undermining the core principles and freedoms of democratic and open societies?

As it happens, yesterday I returned from the Philippines where I participated in a conference of bloggers, activists and citizen journalists from all over the world, people who believe in freedom of expression, the open Internet and multicultural tolerance.

I can tell you terrorists are not the only people who are using social media powerfully and effectively. However, many people connected to this community face serious threats of censorship and imprisonment when they write about subjects or advocate policy positions that their governments find threatening.

In countries like Ethiopia, Russia, Turkey, Egypt, Morocco, China and elsewhere, some have even been charged under broad anti-terror laws that are habitually used as tools to keep incumbent regimes in power.

In response to the tragic massacre in Paris, the French Government has called for United Nations member states to work together on an international legal framework that would place greater responsibility on social networks and other Internet platforms for terrorists' use of their services.

In addressing the problem of terrorists' use of social networking platforms, I believe the United States should adhere to the following principles.

First, multi-stakeholder policymaking. The U.S. opposes U.N. control over Internet governance because many U.N. member states, such as some of the ones that I just listed, advocate policies that would make the Internet much less free and open.

Instead, the U.S. supports a multi-stakeholder approach that includes industry, civil society and the technical community alongside governments in setting policies and technical standards that ensure that the Internet functions globally.

In constructing global responses to terrorists' use of the Internet, we need a multi-stakeholder approach for the same reasons.

Second, any national level laws, regulations or policies aimed at regulating or policing online activities should undergo a human rights risk assessment process to identify potential negative repercussions for freedom of expression, assembly and privacy.

Governments need to be transparent and accountable with the public about the nature and volume of requests being made to companies. Companies need to be able to uphold core principles of freedom of expression and privacy grounded in international human rights standards.

Several major U.S.-based Internet companies have made commitments to uphold these rights as members of the multi-stakeholder Global Network Initiative.

Guidelines for implementing these commitments include narrowly interpreting government demands to restrict content or grant access to user data or communications, challenging government requests that lack a clear legal basis, transparency with users about the types of government requests received and the extent to which the company complies, and restricting compliance to the online domains over which the requesting government actually has jurisdiction.

Third, liability for Internet intermediaries, including social networks, for users' behavior must be kept limited. Research conducted around the world by human rights experts and legal scholars shows clear evidence that when companies are held liable for users' speech and activity, violations of free expression and privacy can be expected to occur as companies preemptively and proactively seek to play it safe and remove anything that might get them in trouble.

Limited liability for Internet companies is an important prerequisite for keeping the Internet open and free.

Fourth, development and enforcement of companies' terms of service and other forms of private policing must also undergo human rights risk assessments.

Any new procedures developed by companies to eliminate terrorist activity from their platforms must be accompanied by engagement with key affected stakeholders, at-risk groups and human rights advocates.

Fifth, in order to prevent abuse and maintain public support for the measures taken, governments as well as companies must provide effective, accessible channels for grievance and remedy for people whose rights to free expression, assembly and privacy have been violated.

Thank you for listening, and I look forward to your questions.

[The prepared statement of Ms. MacKinnon follows:]

Rebecca MacKinnon
Co-Founder, Global Voices Online
Director, Ranking Digital Rights at New America

Testimony to the House Committee on Foreign Affairs
Subcommittee on Terrorism, Nonproliferation, and Trade

"The Evolution of Terrorist Propaganda: The Paris Attack and Social
Media"

January 27, 2015

The democratic world faces a serious challenge: how to fight terrorism and
violent extremism in the Internet age while not undermining the core
principles and freedoms of democratic and open societies.

Yesterday I returned from the Philippines where I participated in a
conference of bloggers, activists, and citizen journalists from all over the
world. Many members of this community face serious threats not only to
their freedom of speech but also to their physical freedom. While some
have been kidnapped or threatened by terrorists or religious extremists,
many more are imprisoned and threatened by governments who have
labeled them terrorists – not because they actually are terrorists under
definitions that people in this hearing room would use, but because they
have expressed views or reported facts that their governments find
threatening.[1]

For example, in Ethiopia a group of bloggers and investigative journalists
known as the "zone nine bloggers" are currently on trial for terrorism under
a law that has frequently been used to silence journalists.[2] Last year the
Russian parliament amended its anti-terror laws to include a set of
draconian Internet controls that justify the jailing of opposition bloggers and
activists, and require companies to keep data of Russian users in Russia
so that they can be better surveilled.[3] In Turkey, the government has

---

[1] http://advocacy.globalvoicesonline.org/2015/01/24/global-voices-calls-for-immediate-release-of-jailed-online-media-workers-and-activists/
[2] http://www.voanews.com/content/court-adjourns-ethiopian-blogger-trial-15-times/2586428.html
[3] https://cpj.org/blog/2014/07/russia-intensifies-restrictions-on-blogs-social-me.php; https://www.aei.org/wp-content/uploads/2015/01/Internet-freedom-in-Putins-Russia.pdf

1

prosecuted journalists for "praising of violence and terrorist propaganda." However an investigation by the Committee to Protect Journalists found that "Turkish authorities conflated the coverage of banned groups and the investigation of sensitive topics with outright terrorism or other anti-state activity."[4] Last year Amnesty International reported that the Moroccan government uses anti-terror laws to target journalists.[5] Egypt has recently made similar use of anti-terror laws.[6]

In response to the tragic Charlie Hebdo massacre in Paris, last week the French government called for UN member states to work together on an international legal framework that would place greater responsibility on social networks and other Internet platforms for terrorist use of their services.[7]

In addressing the problem of terrorist use of social networking platforms, the United States and all other stakeholders committed to upholding international human rights norms, as well as a free and open global Internet, should adhere to the following principles:

1. Multi-stakeholder policymaking

Note that the countries mentioned above that abuse anti-terror laws to jail activists and journalists are all UN member states - along with a long list of other nations including China, Venezuela, and others whose definitions of terrorism are elastic enough to be used to keep incumbent regimes in power. The US has opposed UN control over Internet governance because a large number of UN member states seek a governance framework that would result in a global Internet that is much less free and open than it is today – for commerce and innovation as well as for political discourse. Instead the US supports a multi-stakeholder approach to Internet governance that includes industry, civil society, and the technical community alongside governments in processes that set policies and standards for the global Internet. Any international effort to address terrorism on the Internet should also be grounded in a robust multi-

---

[4] http://cpj.org/2013/02/attacks-on-the-press-misusing-terror-laws.php
[5] http://www.amnesty.org/en/for-media/press-releases/morocco-stop-using-terrorism-pretext-imprison-journalists-2014-05-20
[6] http://www.poynter.org/news/mediawire/250100/mediawireworld-3-journalists-in-egyptian-court-on-world-press-freedom-day/
[7] http://www.reuters.com/article/2015/01/22/us-france-security-internet-idUSKBN0KV2EK20150122

stakeholder approach to ensure that any solutions are compatible with innovation, the free flow of information, and universal human rights.

2. Human rights assessment of laws, regulations, and policies

Any national level laws, regulations, or policies aimed at fighting online terrorism (or any potential regulation affecting online speech or privacy for that matter) should undergo assessment, carried out in consultation with human rights experts and representatives of groups whose rights are potentially at risk of being violated, to identify any ways in which the new measures could have negative consequences for journalism, activism, and the free flow of information more broadly. Policies and laws should not be enacted without robust checks and balances, or if proponents cannot demonstrate how human rights risks will be mitigated.

Laws and regulations governing company actions should be vetted to ensure that they do not compel companies to violate core principles of freedom of expression and privacy, grounded in international human rights standards. Several major US-based Internet companies have made commitments under the multi-stakeholder Global Network Initiative to respect users' freedom of expression and privacy in a number of specific ways. These commitments include: narrowly interpreting government demands to restrict content or grant access to user data or communications; challenging government requests that lack a clear user basis; transparency with users about the types of government requests received and the extent to which the company complies; restricting compliance to the online domains over which the requesting government actually has jurisdiction.[8]

3. Limited intermediary liability.

A large body of research conducted around the world by human rights experts and legal scholars shows clear evidence that when companies are held liable for users' speech and activity, violations of free expression and privacy can be expected to occur for a number of reasons. Companies operating under strict or strong liability regimes generally over-censor in

---

[8] Global Network Initiative Principles: https://globalnetworkinitiative.org//principles/index.php; and Implementation Guidelines: https://globalnetworkinitiative.org//implementationguidelines/index.php

order to avoid legal and regulatory repercussions to their business. Strong liability regimes have also been shown to increase the likelihood that companies will comply with spurious demands for content removal made by governments as well as private parties in order to play it safe: there is no penalty for over-censoring while the legal consequences of under-censoring can be severe.[9] Limited liability for Internet intermediaries is an important prerequisite for keeping the Internet open and free.

4. Transparency, accountability and stakeholder engagement in the development and enforcement of companies' Terms of Service and other forms of self-regulation.

In response to outreach from counter-terrorism authorities among others, some social networking companies are using their terms of service, community guidelines, and other self-regulatory mechanisms to shut down accounts and delete content that is technically protected by the first amendment, or whose removal has not been sought by any government or court through any formal legal process or mechanism. While this may have helped to prevent acts of violent extremism by terrorist groups, there are also many documented cases in which such self-regulation has resulted in censorship of activists, journalists, and political opposition groups. For example last year the SecDev Foundation, a Canadian non-profit that works with digital activists around the world, compiled a list of moderate Syrian opposition groups and citizen journalists whose Facebook pages had been shut down.[10]

More broadly, Facebook has come under fire from activists for enforcing its community guidelines in a way that sometimes silences voices and information that have few other outlets. For example, at the end of last year three Tibetans burned themselves alive to protest Chinese rule. Self-immolation is a gruesome but long-standing form of political protest in

---

[9] Selected sources: *Shielding the Messengers: Protecting Platforms for Expression and Innovation.* Center for Democracy and Technology. December 2012. https://cdt.org/files/pdfs/CDT-Intermediary-Liability-2012.pdf; *Closing the Gap: Indian Online Intermediaries and a Liability System not Fit for Purpose.* March 2014. https://globalnetworkinitiative.org//sites/default/files/Closing%20the%20Gap%20-%20Copenhagen%20Economics_March%202014_0.pdf; *Fostering Freedom Online: The Role of Internet Intermediaries.* UNESCO. December, 2014 http://unesdoc.unesco.org/images/0023/002311/231162e.pdf
[10] http://www.theatlantic.com/international/archive/2014/02/the-syrian-opposition-is-disappearing-from-facebook/283562/

Buddhist societies. The Chinese government censors news of Tibetan protests generally and self immolations in particular. Facebook has deleted postings by Tibetan activists about the recent self-immolations, citing policies forbidding excessively graphic content. Facebook insists that enforcement of its own policies has nothing to do with the Chinese government.[11] While I am inclined to believe them in this case, the point is that de facto political censorship can happen – whether companies intend it or not – when companies lack sufficient mechanisms to ensure transparency about their policies and enforcement practices, and when their policies are developed and implemented without impact assessment or engagement with human rights groups about potential unintended consequences.

Any new self-regulatory mechanisms or procedures developed by companies to combat terror must be accompanied by an increase rather than decrease in the levels of transparency with users and engagement with key affected stakeholders and at-risk groups.

5. Clear and effective grievance and redress mechanisms

In order to prevent abuse of anti-terror laws or informal measures taken by governments or companies, it is vital that there be robust mechanisms and processes for accountability. In particular, governments as well as companies should provide effective, accessible channels for grievance and remedy for people whose rights to free expression, assembly, and privacy have been violated by measures taken to combat online extremism. Public and private entities that abuse these measures in a way that violates human rights must be held accountable.[12]

We live in a time of extraordinary threats to our national security. But the fight against terrorism online must be carried out in a way that also protects and respects human rights. If the US and other democracies cannot figure out how to do this, victories against violent extremism online are likely to be hollow and short lived.

---

[11] http://sinosphere.blogs.nytimes.com/2014/12/27/facebook-deletes-post-on-tibetan-monks-self-immolation/

[12] See the UN Guiding Principles on Business and Human Rights http://www.ohchr.org/Documents/Publications/GuidingPrinciplesBusinessHR_EN.pdf

Mr. POE. I thank all of our panelists for being here. I agree with you, Ms. MacKinnon. This is a very complex issue. I, like everybody else on the dais here, are great believers of the First Amendment.

It is first because it is the most important, and anything Congress does to try to make exceptions is always suspect. But the Immigration and Nationality Act's Section 219 says that no one can aid a foreign terrorist organization.

So we are not talking about some individual who makes some comments on the Internet that is tweeting something. The first requirement is that it is a foreign terrorist organization that is doing this.

It seems to me that that legislation—giving aid to a foreign terrorist organization—was upheld in the Holder v. Humanitarian Law Project in 2010. I think that is the only case where the Supreme Court addressed the issue of Internet, free speech and foreign terrorist organizations.

So we set aside all those other folks out there that are saying things on the Internet—I would like to just address that specific issue—foreign terrorist organization, a member of a foreign terrorist organization, recruiting folks in jihad, radical jihadists to kill other people, like Americans.

What suggestions specifically other than the one Ms. MacKinnon has made—several that she has made—do any of the rest of you have on that specific issue? I know that companies vary and many are, I think, trying to cooperate and bring down these sites on their own.

Mr. Kohlmann, would you like to weigh in on that question? Foreign terrorist organization, member of a foreign terrorist organization, using the Internet to recruit jihadists to kill folks, being very specific about that question.

Mr. KOHLMANN. Sure. I think to the average person, the idea of how would you find terrorist propaganda on Twitter or how to find the important parts, sounds like a gargantuan task.

But the reality is is that the companies we are talking about already have the technology which is capable of doing this without human intervention. And how do I know that?

It is the same reason that when you go on YouTube or Twitter you don't see child pornography. You don't see stolen commercial videos. There is a reason for that. It is not just happenstance.

The reason is because of the fact that the companies that operate those social media platforms have a strict policy when it comes to things like child pornography and stolen copyrighted material and they have proactive means of removing them.

The exact same way that they remove that material they can also remove terrorist propaganda. It is just a matter of switching the search terms, the hash values, the images that they are looking for. The answer is that they don't have an incentive to do that right now.

Mr. POE. And what should that incentive be?

Mr. KOHLMANN. Well, look. Right now there is no legal remedy for anyone in the event that these companies are hosting a terrorist Web site.

I mean, Twitter has never been sued and it has never been held criminally liable or civilly liable by anyone. Why? The answer is because of the fact that—the way that it is right now—Internet hosting provider law is written so that an Internet hosting provider, if they don't have active knowledge of what is going on, they are not really responsible.

And look, I don't want to crack down on the freedom of speech and I don't want to make Internet companies responsible for everything that their users do, when there are some things that their users do we will never really be able to know about.

But there is a certain level of basic responsibility that companies like Twitter and CloudFlare are failing to meet. We are not asking that they find every single terrorist Web site or they shut down every single terrorist video, just to make a best effort. And anyone who says that the effort that is being made right now is a best effort has no idea what they are talking about.

Mr. POE. Okay. I have a question for you, Ambassador. Once again, I am talking specifically not about terrorists. I am talking about members of a foreign terrorist organization, which the law specifically addresses currently.

Ambassador Wallace, the FBI follows these chats and they don't seem to encourage the bringing down of some of this Internet material because they want to follow the bad guys all over the world, what they are saying, who they are, et cetera.

What is your reaction to that?

Mr. WALLACE. I think it is very clear that the intelligence value of having everything open and accessible is incredibly overstated. It is very much like, with due respect, the demagoguery associated that somehow we are all talking about impairing First Amendment rights.

All of us support the First Amendment here but this isn't free speech. This is hate speech, and I think that, having previously served in our Government and having been a consumer of our intelligence data, we have so many good tools that allow us to track terrorists' activity that we don't need to solely rely on the open forums.

The value of taking down these recruiters, these propagandizers, far exceeds the intelligence value that we would get from fully tracking all the individual users of social media.

So I think it is very clear. Maybe at one point when there were only a few abusers a long time ago there might have been intelligence value. But right now, the Internet is awash with those that would propagandize, recruit and incite terror. We have to take these down, and as J.M. said, it matters. It has an effect.

Mr. POE. The Chair will yield to the ranking member 5 minutes for his questions of the panel.

Mr. KEATING. Thank you, Mr. Chairman.

One area, and I would initially do it with Mr. Berger because he alluded to metrics that were used themselves, but in your analysis, and I will throw it open to the other witnesses as well, part of the difficulty will be—you know, the chairman set one specific example but as you go along it becomes a little more difficult.

What material, you know, and to what extent when you were looking at your metrics did you draw the line in some of these postings to have them fit into your analysis? You had to draw a line somewhere if you had metrics.

Can you give us some examples of what, in your analysis, was on one side of the line and what was on the other?

Mr. BERGER. So for this particular paper what we wanted to do was——

Mr. POE. Would you speak up a little bit, please?

Mr. BERGER. Sure. I don't know if—okay.

Mr. POE. I am just a little deaf so talk louder, Mr. Berger.

Mr. BERGER. For this particular paper what we did was we wanted to identify people who were specifically ISIS supporters and not supporters of other jihadist groups.

So what we developed was a metric to sort the 50,000 accounts we had really robust information on and we evaluated them based on whether they appeared to be interested in just ISIS and whether they were promoting ISIS or whether they were more broadly interested in following jihadist activity.

So in this case, we got very, very specific. What I will say about the intelligence question and the metrics in this kind of material is relevant to that it is possible to sift out the noise on here.

So we did a demographic study that we will publish in detail on 20,000 ISIS supporters. But within that group it is eminently possible to zero in on who the media people are, on who the foreign fighters are, who is in the country, who is not in the country.

You know, the issue that you run into with this is that you can't do it 100 percent. So we created a sample group to do our demographics as 20,000 accounts that is 95 percent ISIS supporters.

So if you are going to approach this problem legislatively or encourage companies to take a more aggressive role, one of the things you have to do is figure out first where you are going to draw the line, whether it is going to be a member of the organization. There aren't 20,000 ISIS members on Twitter. There are 20,000 ISIS supporters that we can point to.

So how much involvement do they have to have and how are we going to determine that without going in with a search warrant and really getting, you know, very invasive about how we are going to get that information out of the company.

Mr. KEATING. So you did it based on, you know, people that you identified through your analysis as ISIS. Can I just be a little more broader and thematic in this?

Can you give me any examples just off the top of your head where it is clear, you know, where you are on one side of the line where it is a difficult choice, and the other side of the line when it isn't? Because those are the kind of decisions——

Mr. BERGER. Sure.

Mr. KEATING [continuing]. We might have to do it, and I would ask anyone if they wanted to venture in. Ms. MacKinnon, did you get a chance? Where would you say—can you give an example where it is clearly an issue where action should be taken and it is one where even though it might be a close call it is not?

Ms. MACKINNON. I am not a counter terrorism expert so I am not going to go outside of my field of expertise. But I, certainly, can say that the question is: Who is going to make the determination where the line is drawn, right? Is it the company? Is it the government? Is it someone else? Is it an outside expert?

Mr. KEATING. And do they use a common——

Ms. MACKINNON. And in order to determine what side of the line this person falls on, is the company going to need to conduct an investigation of that person and where they are coming from?

This leads to an issue of there is already a great public backlash about the amount of information that companies are collecting on people and the way in which it is shared with law enforcement and national security.

And so companies, in thinking about not just their domestic trust with users but their trust with international users which is the main growth area for all of these companies, are they going to have to start building their own profiles on, you know, users of interest in order to decide which side of the line they fall on.

Mr. KEATING. Okay. Let me just ask the other witnesses that we have. What could we do to establish those kind of guidelines that would be useful from company to company? Can it be done in a uniform way?

Mr. WALLACE. Sure, I will take a quick crack. Look, the clear line to us is incitement of violence, right? I mean, there are a lot of lawyers in the room. Incitement of violence, clearly, or terror is clear.

Threatening to behead Fran Townsend on Twitter, I think, shouldn't be on Twitter. I think that is very clear and constitutes a bright line. I think we would all agree that shouldn't be there.

Mr. KEATING. But where it gets a little gray?

Mr. WALLACE. Where it gets a little bit gray is saying that you support these groups. I would say that now is the time to change. Inspire magazine is a classic example.

This is a publication that has been providing material support for al-Qaeda for a long time. We have been tolerating it under the right of free expression.

There is an excellent op-ed in the New York Times I think 2 days ago that said, "No more al-Qaeda magazines." I think now we can say that as it pertains to terrorist organizations, we have taken a decision that promoting these groups is a violation of law.

We should not tolerate hate speech that supports these entities and we shouldn't allow the Internet versions of Inspire magazine.

Mr. KEATING. All right. I will just have this one comment, Mr. Chairman, and yield back. The answers were basically group centered, and when it comes to that we have to move forward somehow and grasp the content—maybe we will deal with that in a second round.

I yield back, Mr. Chair.

Mr. POE. The Chair will recognize the gentleman from South Carolina, Mr. Wilson, for 5 minutes.

Mr. WILSON. Thank you, Mr. Chairman.

I thank all of you for being here today and I want to thank you, Ambassador, for pointing out the circumstances of Whac-A-Mole because it seems like that is where we are. Then you proceeded that we can be successful and have been in blocking child pornography, drug sales, human trafficking.

And, Mr. Kohlmann, thank you for pointing out about stolen copyrighted material. There is hope, and for the American people we need this because respecting, indeed, as Ms. MacKinnon has pointed out, the First Amendment rights that we so respect, certainly, that doesn't include promoting mass murder.

And I just sincerely hope that with the good minds who are here that, indeed, positive programs can be developed. In fact, Ambassador, could you tell us about the Think Again campaign and has there been success or limitations based on that particular program by the State Department?

Mr. WALLACE. You know, there are various tools in the toolshed. One of them is the counter narrative argument and that has been the State Department's effort of trying to win the war of ideas.

At the Counter Extremism Project, we take the position that we should be pursuing all items on the menu, order every item on the menu. And the counter-narrative option is important. Obviously, the State Department has had some fumbling around initially with the Think Again program; it has had some difficulty. Our focus right now is there are many tens of thousands of these actors on the Internet.

I think if we focused on the seed accounts, those that are really driving this conversation, and work cooperatively with the online platforms and systematically took them down, it would provide opportunities for the State Department and others to engage in legitimate counter narrative conversations because they would have the advantage of not having the jihadis online.

So I think this is something that we need to do collectively and collaboratively.

Mr. WILSON. And, to me, it is so important that we counter the brainwashing messages that are utterly bizarre. A couple years ago I was in Pakistan and I was reading a newspaper that was very vibrant and seemed very positive and very open minded, and then I read an op-ed and it was accusing the United States of intentionally targeting mosques and all kind of bizarre accusations that had no basis at all in reality.

And then I looked to see who the author of the article was: Fidel Castro. How would he know this? It was an utter fabrication. And so whoever would like to answer, how are our governments and civil service organizations using social media platforms to counter terrorist messaging and propaganda?

Mr. KOHLMANN. I would just say this. I would say that it is a great thing to counter terrorist propaganda. I would say that thus far the efforts of the State Department and social media to do this have not been very successful, and I can tell you that from directly studying them.

Most of the time when State Department social media representatives get involved on jihadi forums or any forums that have people from the Middle East on them they have to identify themselves, first of all, as being State Department representatives, and that kind of ends the discussion right there because the rest of the people then start spouting off about—why is America sticking its nose in our business, and why are there spies observing our conversations and what not.

So that program by and large, in my opinion, is a complete failure. The most successful single thing we can do to counter their ideology is show where the rubber meets the road. And what do I mean by that?

Right now, ISIS and al-Qaeda, in particular AQAP, right now they are locked in this test of wills where they are putting out nasty, nasty stuff about each other on the Internet in English and Arabic and all sorts of languages.

ISIS just put out a whole magazine in which they accused al-Qaeda and the Taliban of being deviant morons. Now, that is what needs to go out there. That is what we need to be rebroadcasting, the fact that these guys think that each other are a bunch of clowns.

There is no honor in this. There is no courage or valor. They both think that they are idiots, and if you put that out there and you show that these guys are really amateurs, they are clowns, that most of the people that are involved in this don't even believe in the ideology, that is where you really crack the seal.

That is where you start breaking the hold that these folks have in social media. You have to show that they are full of it, and they are, and the only way you can do that is by showing their own videos in which they are massacring people, massacring Muslims.

There is no explanation for that anywhere in their propaganda. You have to show that. That is what weakens them.

Mr. WILSON. Well, again, thank you, and—to show the truth. Thank you so much and, indeed, how sad it is that the chief victims of what is going on are fellow Muslims first. We seem to be second. Thank you.

Mr. POE. The Chair recognizes the gentleman from California, Mr. Sherman, for 5 minutes.

Mr. SHERMAN. I want to focus first on getting our message out. The Internet as a tool favors the side that is trying to get information out and puts grave, both legal questions and technological questions, and just Whac-A-Mole difficulties on somebody who is trying to keep information from getting out. So if we can get our message to defeat their message the technology is with us.

I want to bring to the attention of this subcommittee something I have mentioned, I think, in the full committee and that is the State Department refuses to hire a single Islamic expert, not a single person who is really qualified to quote Hadith and Koranic verses. Not one.

And so we are in a circumstance where we think the best argument to use on those who are close to embracing Islamic extremism is to say they kill children, isn't that obviously bad?

Well, in the world of Islamic extremists maybe that is not one of the top 10 sins. If we had some understanding of basic Islam and then extremist Islam from people who are not just passing knowledge but are people who have memorized the Koran then we can do a much better job.

But that would mean taking State Department jobs away or at least one away from people with fancy degrees from U.S. and the Western European universities, and it has been completely rejected by the State Department, who thinks they are going to make arguments thought of in our minds to people of a completely different mindset.

So, I mean, these are folks who barely know enough not to hold a get-together with ham sandwiches and beer to discuss what Islam does not allow, okay?

Mr. Kohlmann, do they have the technology not only to deactivate a particular user but to deactivate that IP address, that computer, so that they can't just log in from that particular site and give a different name?

Mr. KOHLMANN. One hundred percent, and——

Mr. SHERMAN. Do they use it?

Mr. KOHLMANN. No, and I—that is——

Mr. SHERMAN. Wait a minute. So you go online and you put up something so bad that Twitter actually does take you down.

Mr. KOHLMANN. They don't ban the IP, no.

Mr. SHERMAN. You eat lunch, you go back on, you use the same computer to put up similar material but you identify yourself as, you know, with a different name and they leave you up?

Mr. KOHLMANN. There is a jihadist that just commented the other day. He actually tweeted at Twitter and said why don't you just stop this pantomime and stop doing this whole thing where you shut down our accounts occasionally; it just takes us 2 minutes to create a new account when you shut one down. They——

Mr. SHERMAN. And they can do it from the same computer? Okay.

Mr. KOHLMANN. Yes. Twitter doesn't look at these kind of things because, again, they don't have any incentive to.

Mr. SHERMAN. Well, that raises the next issue and that is how do we put the right kind of pressure on these organizations. At a minimum, this subcommittee ought to be involved in naming and shaming.

But then you go beyond that to perhaps changing our tax laws, which doesn't raise some of the same First Amendment arguments, or otherwise penalizing those that carry the message at least when the author is an identified foreign terrorist organization, because that doesn't require delving into content and parsing words.

Even if it is just weather reports from Mosul, if they are brought to you by ISIS, they shouldn't be on Twitter. Just to give you an illustration of how difficult it is to get our law enforcement authorities to take seriously anything that is a few steps away from the dead body, something that is in the realm of finance and propaganda, I brought to the attention of Eric Holder himself a video showing Americans in Orange County raising money for Hamas.

They still haven't even lost their tax exemption so we are subsidizing it, and the Americans who were on the flotilla that took building materials to Gaza and turned them over to Hamas, not even a letter of inquiry.

So we live in this world where, yes, if we see you with a gun or a bomb we know you are a threat but if you violate our clearest laws but you are white collar, we don't want to do anything.

So I realize it is going to be tougher to get these, to force by rule of law taking down certain messages because, where do you draw the line between those who advocate for ISIS and those who say, well, ISIS isn't quite as bad as Brad Sherman says they are?

But we can certainly take down anything that claims, whether it is true or not, to be posting to a foreign terrorist organization. Ms. MacKinnon, you haven't commented. You have been an advocate for privacy here. Why not just take it down if it says brought to you by any organization on the U.S. foreign terrorist organization list?

Ms. MACKINNON. Well, I think at root here we have a trust problem that is going three ways. I think that there has been sort of a history over the last couple of years of Internet companies, particularly in light of the Snowden revelations, of feeling that they need to restore trust with their users in terms of what kinds of information they are handing over to the government, what kinds of requests they are responding to and so there is an incentive on the part of the companies not to comply further.

Mr. SHERMAN. My time has expired. But if these rich companies making a fortune can't lose a few percentage points on their profit to help us in the war on terrorism, there is something the matter with their souls, and I yield back.

Mr. POE. The Chair will recognize the gentleman from Texas, Mr. Castro, for 5 minutes.

Mr. CASTRO. Thank you, Chairman Poe. Thank you to each of the panelists who are here to testify before us. We appreciate you being here and your sharing your wisdom.

You know, I think, like most Americans, after there is an attack in Paris, for example, the Boston bombing, and we see people take credit for that on Twitter—one of the social media sites—you ask yourself, you know, why the hell do these people have a Twitter account or a Facebook account. I think that is what the average American thinks.

So I certainly support asking Twitter to be cooperative in developing protocols to make sure that we root some of this stuff out, as you have suggested, that Facebook and others have. And so I have a few questions, though.

Have they done that for any nation? Are there different rules in the United States versus Europe, for example, or somewhere else?

Mr. KOHLMANN. As far as I am aware, there are no different rules in terms of terrorist organizations. It really seems—especially, at least as we take the example of Twitter. Twitter, generally speaking, only takes action when there is a public embarrassment, when there is a public spectacle. So when the James Foley video came out, all of a sudden you see public comments from Jack Dorsey.

You see Twitter all of a sudden rashly knocking out a whole bunch of accounts, and then all of a sudden silence for months. Then, all of a sudden, there will be a new video that will make it to a front page headline on CNN or MSNBC, and then once again Twitter will go on a rampage for a week. But, again, that is just for——

Mr. CASTRO. Let me ask Ms. MacKinnon and anyone can chime in.

Ms. MACKINNON. Sure. Yes. A lot of these companies—Twitter, Facebook and Google, in particular, that I have some familiarity with—generally have policies around the world where they will, in countries where they have operations, respond to lawful requests—so requests that are made in accordance with local law officially, you know, in writing.

Mr. CASTRO. Right.

Ms. MACKINNON. But if those requests do not have legal basis in that jurisdiction, they will not comply. Then, of course, they have terms of service that restrict speech that may or may not be legal in a given place.

Mr. CASTRO. Well, I guess, and I think this is a tough question because the United States and Americans, obviously, value the First Amendment a lot and you have to start making a distinction between what crosses over from speech to getting closer to expression and action.

For example, I know that somebody on the panel made the comment that this is hate speech and I would agree that a lot of it is. But there is a lot of hate speech on the Internet.

And so, for example, how do you make the distinction between Islamic terrorism and domestic terrorism? When there were thousands of children who were coming across the U.S.-Mexico border, turning themselves over to Border Patrol, there were organized militias that were organizing on Twitter and Facebook and all the social media sites to go down there with arms, with weapons, and a few of them had confrontation with law enforcement.

So how do you draw that distinction? Or are we just going to say as Americans we are going to do it for Islamic terrorism but we are not going to draw a line for domestic terrorism?

I think those are some of the tough questions that we have got to answer among ourselves. And, like I said, I support movement and action on this issue. I think it is prudent. But there are some very deep and very tough questions that we need to answer.

Mr. BERGER. I just wanted to say there are some precedents for this. I mean, so, for instance, France has a law against anti-Semitic speech and Twitter was complying with that law to provide information on users.

You know, the other thing that I think is not necessarily informing the conversation we are having here right now is that Facebook, YouTube and Twitter do cooperate with law enforcement requests to some extent and they do take accounts down based on government requests, to some extent.

One reason we don't know about that is because a lot of that happens under national security letters and other forms of requests that they are not allowed to disclose, and one thing that would help us understand this better is if they were allowed to have a little more transparency about——

Mr. CASTRO. Sure. Maybe let Ambassador Wallace also.

Mr. WALLACE. Good to see you, Congressman.

Mr. CASTRO. Yes.

Mr. WALLACE. Look, I fully agree. But I don't think that we need to reinvent the definition of hate speech in this hearing. There has been an entire body of constitutional law that has developed around hate speech and that has been pretty clear.

So I agree with you, sir, that hate speech is hate speech. It should come down and we should take action on hate speech. It shouldn't be allowed.

But I think we are looking for a bright line, Mr. Keating. You know, I think that the distinction of the well-developed law on hate speech is take down those that are designated terrorist organizations, those that provide material support, whether it is ideological or otherwise, we have said that those actors are doing things that are hateful, for lack of a better——

Mr. CASTRO. Designated by the United States Government?

Mr. WALLACE. Correct. Correct. And I think that it should be without doubt that if it is an AQAP supporter or an ISIS supporter or Inspire magazine, they should come down now. But I fully agree with you, Congressman. You know, hate speech is hate speech.

Mr. CASTRO. Can I ask one more question?

Mr. POE. Sure.

Mr. CASTRO. But would you put the same restrictions on an organization that is going to recruit another Timothy McVeigh or Terry Nichols?

Mr. WALLACE. Yes.

Mr. CASTRO. Well, but that is not part of this conversation, right?

Mr. WALLACE. Well——

Mr. CASTRO. So you start getting into a broader—and I agree. I just think you start getting into a broader conversation of moving it beyond Islamic terrorism into domestic terrorism also.

Mr. WALLACE. Right. I mean, Congressman, you and I have spent much time together. I think everyone agrees on the nature of bad actors like Timothy McVeigh.

But right now, we have to be honest with ourselves that the grave national security concern, the threat to global security, are these cyber jihadis that are propagandizing.

I certainly don't want to minimize in any way that the next Timothy McVeigh that we should allow him to stand or somebody else who would brutally seek to harm lawful or unlawful immigrants.

We shouldn't. But, obviously, the focus right now has been because of—there are so many examples. So I don't mean to diminish——

Mr. CASTRO. Sure. No, no, no.

Mr. WALLACE [continuing]. Those examples in any way, sir, and I fully agree with you, of course.

Mr. CASTRO. Yes. Sure. Thank you.

Mr. POE. The gentleman yields back. We are in the middle of votes. One last comment, then I will yield to the ranking member for a final comment as well.

The law makes a distinction between a foreign terrorist organization and non-organization using the Internet including domestic terrorist organizations. Those types of organizations, my understanding, you cannot provide any assistance, even helpful assistance.

Like in the Holder v. Humanitarian Law Project, they weren't advocating terrorism. They were advocating peace. But the Supreme Court said you cannot assist a foreign terrorist organization and it is a violation of the Section 219 of the law whether it is peace or advocating jihadist movements, and I think Congress has an obligation to look into this whole matter and try to see if we need to get involved.

As Mr. Berger pointed out, some of these organizations—Google, for example—are doing what they can when asked to or on their own to take down some of these sites. Twitter, not so much.

But I appreciate all four of you being here and the comments, I think, by the panelists and by the members were excellent. And I will yield the last comment—give you the last word, something I never do.

Mr. KEATING. Never done, and I appreciate that. I am sure it is just because it is my first hearing.

Mr. POE. It is.

Mr. KEATING. I just want to thank—this has been an important hearing, I think, and a frustrating one because it is sort of like trying to grasp a watermelon seed. Once you think you have it, it slips through your fingers again.

But it is important to begin this dialogue, and there are some areas, I have learned today, that can be helpful where maybe we can limit to specific, you know, groups or individuals and not get involved in some of the other issues.

But even that becomes complex because the difficulty of dealing with different languages, different laws and different countries makes it become very difficult.

But I think one thing we can agree on it is important for us all going forward to try and get our hands around this a little bit and to see what we can do, whether it is hate speech or existing law.

But, you know, you have got companies. You are their guests on those—you know, of those companies as well. So I think that working with the private side, having those discussions, will really serve a great benefit and I hope today was a time that we can refocus on this from such a broad perspective, as frustrating as the conversation was. Thank you all for being here.

Mr. POE. I thank all four of you for being here. It is very important information you have given us. I thank the members for participating as well, and the subcommittee is adjourned. Thank you very much.

[Whereupon, at 3:50 p.m., the committee was adjourned.]

APPENDIX

---

(75)

SUBCOMMITTEE HEARING NOTICE
COMMITTEE ON FOREIGN AFFAIRS
U.S. HOUSE OF REPRESENTATIVES
WASHINGTON, DC 20515-6128

Subcommittee on Terrorism, Nonproliferation, and Trade

Ted Poe (R-TX), Chairman

TO: MEMBERS OF THE COMMITTEE ON FOREIGN AFFAIRS

You are respectfully requested to attend an OPEN hearing of the Committee on Foreign Affairs, to be held by the Subcommittee on Terrorism, Nonproliferation, and Trade in Room 2172 of the Rayburn House Office Building (and available live on the Committee website at http://www.ForeignAffairs.house.gov):

DATE: Tuesday, January 27, 2015

TIME: 2:30 p.m.

SUBJECT: The Evolution of Terrorist Propaganda: The Paris Attack and Social Media

WITNESSES: The Honorable Mark Wallace
                   Chief Executive Officer
                   Counter Extremism Project

                   Mr. J.M. Berger
                   Author

                   Mr. Evan Kohlmann
                   Chief Information Officer
                   Flashpoint Partners

                   Ms. Rebecca MacKinnon
                   Director, Ranking Digital Rights
                   New America

By Direction of the Chairman

The Committee on Foreign Affairs seeks to make its facilities accessible to persons with disabilities. If you are in need of special accommodations, please call 202/225-5021 at least four business days in advance of the event, whenever practicable. Questions with regard to special accommodations in general (including availability of Committee materials in alternative formats and assistive listening devices) may be directed to the Committee.

COMMITTEE ON FOREIGN AFFAIRS

MINUTES OF SUBCOMMITTEE ON _____ *Terrorism Nonproliferation and Trade* _____ HEARING

Day ___ *Tuesday* ___ Date ___ *January 27, 2015* ___ Room ___ *2172* ___

Starting Time ___ *2:30 p.m.* ___ Ending Time ___ *3:50 p.m.* ___

Recesses |____| (____ to ____) (____ to ____) (____ to ____) (____ to ____) (____ to ____) (____ to ____)

Presiding Member(s)

Chairman Ted Poe

Check all of the following that apply:

Open Session ☑
Executive (closed) Session ☐
Televised ☑

Electronically Recorded (taped) ☑
Stenographic Record ☑

TITLE OF HEARING:

"The Evolution of Terrorist Propaganada: The Paris Attack and Social Media"

SUBCOMMITTEE MEMBERS PRESENT:

Reps. Poe, Wilson, Cook, Keating, Sherman, and Castro

NON-SUBCOMMITTEE MEMBERS PRESENT: *(Mark with an * if they are not members of full committee.)*

HEARING WITNESSES: Same as meeting notice attached? Yes ☑ No ☐
(If "no", please list below and include title, agency, department, or organization.)

STATEMENTS FOR THE RECORD: *(List any statements submitted for the record.)*

TIME SCHEDULED TO RECONVENE _____
or
TIME ADJOURNED ___ *3:50 p.m.* ___

_____
Subcommittee Staff Director

www.ingramcontent.com/pod-product-compliance
Lightning Source LLC
Chambersburg PA
CBHW080517290526
45790CB00006B/2198